HAMLET

In Defense of the Faith

PATRICIA GEANEY KERRIGAN

ISBN: 978-1-955119-37-5 (Paperback)
ISBN: 978-1-955119-38-2 (Ebook)

LCCN: 2022908802
Published by: Milibrat Press
Cover Designer: Michelle Fairbanks

CONTENTS

ACKNOWLEDGEMENTS

I t is with true gratitude that I thank my husband Patrick for his encouragement and support in the writing of this book. I appreciate his sharing my interest in *Hamlet*, his probing questions that led to a greater understanding of the play, and his valuable feedback to every section of the book as I wrote it.

Our son Patrick's much appreciated gift, in 2001, of two tickets to a production of *Hamlet* started the discussion that led almost twenty years later to the writing of this book. His valuable suggestions on ways to strengthen the final draft were greatly appreciated.

Ann-Marie, our daughter, shared her assessment of an early draft. Her thoughtful analysis of the work's strengths and weaknesses was especially helpful and very much appreciated. Her positive reaction at that early stage was most encouraging.

Our daughter Katherine supported not only my writing effort, but, also, during the stress of the pandemic, heartened all of us, and her own family, with the joy, humor, optimism, and hopefulness that are consistently hers.

I am sincerely grateful, as well, to Maureen Floryan, a friend and fellow former English teacher. Her reading of my manuscript, and her positive reaction to it, meant a great deal and encouraged me to do something with what I had written.

PREFACE

Several factors came together to create the end result of this book. The first was that our son, Patrick, gave my husband Patrick and me tickets to a Royal National Theatre performance of *Hamlet* on April 21, 2001, at the Wilbur Theatre in Boston.

After raising a family, I had returned to full time teaching a few years before. Each year when I taught *Hamlet* to my 12th grade English classes, my family heard me extol the virtues of the play.

After the play, my husband asked, "Why the Roman names?" A week later he wanted to know if Shakespeare could have been Catholic.

My immediate response to my husband was that Shakespeare would not have been. However, my husband persisted, and I went to my college textbook, *SHAKESPEARE Twenty-three Plays and the Sonnets*, and discovered that Shakespeare's mother's family, the Arden's of Warwickshire, were believed to have held on to their Roman Catholic beliefs. From that point, the play began quickly to take on a whole new significance.

Until then, I had viewed Prince Hamlet as idealistic with a sterling character, but as having grown disillusioned and cynical. I saw him, and all the characters, as not only affected by the poison of Claudius's evil, but as infected as well. I had seen a distinct pattern of reason, conscience, will in the play, and had pointed out in my classes how Claudius and Hamlet were equal in reason and conscience, but differed in the strength of their will.

I had noted the playwright's reference to Saint Patrick, and had wondered why the Irish saint was invoked. I had observed the religious elements of purgatory, confession, the chalice of wine, yet had not seen any distinct religious meaning to the play.

However, as a result of my husband's questions, I reviewed the main facts of the English Reformation and quickly became convinced that the play was, in fact, an allegory, and that Claudius represented Henry VIII. It was as if a veil started to lift, and the details began to fit into a pattern. Claudius's "incestuous" marriage alluded to Henry's marriage to Catherine of Aragon, as well as to the union between Church and State, a union too close, when Henry made himself head of the Church in England. The "o'er hasty marriage" of Claudius to Gertrude represented the nullification of Henry's marriage to Catherine, the validation of his marriage to Anne Boleyn, and Anne's coronation, all within a month.

The Jesuits having been instrumental during the Counter-Reformation, I began to think that Hamlet's quick-witted insult to Claudius of being too much "in the sun" was also an allusion to the Seal of the Society of Jesus. I became convinced that there was indeed a Jesuit "overlay" to the play when I bought a copy of *The Spiritual Exercises of Saint Ignatius* and realized that the play paralleled the pattern of reason, conscience, will in *The Exercises*.

Each year when I taught *Hamlet* to my 12th grade classes, I saw more evidence in the text to support the allegorical interpretation, although as a teacher in a public school, I made no reference to it in the classroom. Having also taught *Macbeth, Othello,* and *King Lear,* I suspected all the great tragedies reinforced the meaning of *Hamlet.*

Although I became more aware of speculation that Shakespeare may indeed have had Catholic leanings, I became equally interested in the Marlovian theory of Christopher Marlowe being the playwright, faking his death, being spirited out of England, sending the plays back to England, and of Shakespeare introducing them to the London stage.

In 2008, when I retired from teaching, I figured I would have time to write down some of my thoughts on the play. However, our first grandchild was born that year, and more grandchildren quickly followed. My husband and I began traveling, and so, though I kept saying I really intended to sit down and write, it did not happen.

The reference to Saint Patrick had continued to intrigue me. I thought there was more significance to it than the usual explanation that it is an allusion to Saint Patrick's Purgatory, a well in Ireland. In line with the allegorical interpretation, I took the reference to Saint Patrick to mean that, with Henry VIII usurping the Apostolic Authority of the Church, there had been great "offense" to Christianity. Therefore, my interest in Saint Patrick was greatly piqued.

In 2002, I discovered the book *PATRICK The Pilgrim Apostle of Ireland* in a bookstore, purchased it, and read only portions, looking mostly for biographical information on Saint Patrick. In April 2002, on a trip to Florida, my husband and I attended Mass at the Basilica of Mary, Queen of the Universe in Orlando. To my surprise, the priest announced that the author of that same book on Saint Patrick, Sister Maire de Paor (Sr. Declan), an Irish scholar and member of the Presentation Order, would be signing copies and speaking in the Basilica's gift shop after Mass. I have kept the flyer advertising her talk, which I had asked her to sign, as my copy of the book was back home in Massachusetts. Ironically, her book would sit mostly unread until this past summer during the pandemic.

On a trip to Italy in 2013, I discovered, in a bookstore in Venice, the book *The Shakespeare Guide to Italy* by Richard Paul Roe. I did not purchase it then, but did in September 2020, when I became curious about Roe's theories on the playwright's travels in Italy.

At the beginning of the pandemic, finding myself distracted and restless, I looked around for something especially engaging to read. A few years before retiring, I had purchased Stephen Greenblatt's *Hamlet in Purgatory*, but had not read it in full. This time I did.

Dusting one morning, while still immersed in reading Greenblatt, I took Sr. Declan's book on Saint Patrick off the bookshelf and left it on a table, thinking I might pick it up after Greenblatt. When, finally, I did, it was late summer 2020. At last, in the midst of the pandemic, I delved fully into *PATRICK The Pilgrim Apostle of Ireland*, a scholarly analysis of the writings of Saint Patrick. Finally, I read the full texts of Saint Patrick's ancient writings, included at the end of Sr. Declan's book. Previously, I had read only part of *Confessio*, and none of *Epistola*.

As I discussed what I was reading with my husband, he asked further questions. Why Denmark? Why the name "The Mousetrap"? Why the name Gonzago? His prompting me to look up the word revenge led to realization of what really was intended by the Ghost's command. My husband's questions, starting in 2001, pushed me to probe more deeply, and led me to understand more fully.

What I discovered by reading the ancient writings of Saint Patrick convinced me finally to sit down and write.

Patricia Geaney Kerrigan

April 6, 2021

INTRODUCTION

Hamlet not only has been appreciated by audiences for centuries; it is one of the most analyzed works of literature. Many have studied, pondered the depths of its meaning, yet perhaps have sensed that as much as is said about it, there remains more to be said. Something about the play remains elusive. What really is Shakespeare saying about human nature, England, religion, his historical moment in time, or the nature of tragedy? More so than other profound and masterful works, there are elements of *Hamlet* which seem not quite fully or satisfactorily explained. Further mystifying *Hamlet* aficionados is the question of whether Shakespeare is indeed the author of the play. This book will demonstrate that the play does, in fact, have one clear and discernible message, that it is an allegory, that it has Jesuitical overtones, and will, furthermore, suggest that someone other than Shakespeare wrote the plays attributed to him.

There has been much speculation about the playwright's religion. Was he a recusant Catholic? In Elizabethan England, he would not have been able to admit so openly. Recusant Catholics faced heavy fines, imprison-ment, even death. Certainly, he would not have been free to produce on the London stage a play that affirmed Roman Catholic belief.

Or would he have been? Critics acknowledge certain echoes of the old Faith in *Hamlet*. Clearly the Ghost has come from purgatory, a doctrine of the Church that the Church of England had renounced. Hamlet tells Ophelia to get to a nunnery, yet under Henry VIII the monasteries had been closed and laid to ruin. Claudius, on his knees, seeks to confess but cannot repent for his sin; the English Church no longer considered Penance a sacrament. The chalice of wine that Claudius has prepared for Hamlet, and from which Gertrude drinks, is a poisoned cup. The Protestant communion cup, not transubstantiated into the Body and Blood of Christ, would have, according to recusant Catholics, offered no spiritual nourishment.

With so much pertaining to Roman Catholicism rever-berating through the play, it is not too difficult to conjecture that the play might have allegorical meaning, some insight on faith, or even on England's break with the Church of Rome. What that point might be, however, could be open to interpretation. Therefore, critics often look beyond the text of the play for answers. Should they not, rather, assume that this play that engages the mind so masterfully, must have acute, not ambiguous, meaning, and must be so well crafted that all necessary clues to that meaning are in the text?

The clues, to be certain, are there, just not obvious. The most essential are those most easily overlooked. They are not given their due because they are allusions and parallels to two ancient texts, works themselves overlooked for centuries: the fifth century writings of Saint Patrick, entitled *Confessio* and *Epistola*. The parallels between these works and *Hamlet* make very clear and certain what the point is of the play.

Confessio is Saint Patrick's defense against false allegations brought against him by certain clergy in Britain; it is his testimony to his faith, and it is especially his legacy to the faithful in Ireland. *Epistola*, written earlier, is Saint Patrick's letter to Coroticus, a British chieftain, condemning him for having raided the coast of Ireland, and having captured, murdered, and sold into captivity, newly baptized Christians.

With Patrick's *Epistola* in hand, it becomes almost impossible not to see *Hamlet* as an allegory denouncing Henry VIII for making himself head of the Church in England in order to divorce Catherine and marry Anne Boleyn, thus usurping, and breaking from, the authority of the Church. Roman Catholics in England, like the captured Irish Christians, were held captive, unable to practice their faith without retribution.

By the time *Hamlet* was written, sometime between 1599 and 1602, the faith as practiced in England had deviated significantly from doctrine of the early Church and pre-Reformation Western Christianity. In fact, in the Great Schism of 1054, Eastern and Western Christianity had remained far more in agreement on doctrine than did the Protestant Reformation with traditional Christianity, which, for a millennium, had remained unified.

The Schism broke Christianity into two parts. The Reformation, almost five hundred years later, splintered it into many parts, and ushered in considerable divergence in what Christians believed.

The Church's unity rested on the foundations of Sacred Tradition and the Old and New Testaments, the sources of Christian orthodoxy. From the fourth century, once Constantine made Christianity legal, and it spread quickly throughout the Roman Empire, the Church had guarded against heresy. Even when East and West split, each remained steadfast in belief in the Real Presence in the Eucharist (bread and wine becoming materially the Body and Blood of Christ), the sacraments, Sacred Tradition, justification by faith and works. In the sixteenth century, when reformers broke from the Church, they renounced doctrine to which believers since the early Christians had adhered.

It was at this time of cataclysmic break in Church unity, and of danger to those in England who continued to practice their faith, not conforming to the official religion, that *Hamlet* was introduced to the London stage. In Elizabethan England, under the Act of Uniformity, weekly attendance at Church of England services was made mandatory, and attendance at Catholic Mass was outlawed.

It is imperative, therefore, that we judge the play not by our modern sensibilities, nor by our personal religious biases, but by the context of its own time. We must seek to understand the meaning that the author intended and purposely crafted with his words in response to the age in which he lived.

For the playwright to condemn the Crown on the open stage would have been possible only if the allegorical message was hinted at, but not certain unless one was familiar with Saint Patrick's ancient texts.

The parallels between, the allusions to, and the echoes of *Confessio*, and especially *Epistola*, in the play are so convincing that one has surely to realize they are there by design. If the meaning of the play was to remind the English of the Faith they once had, and had lost, and if the play was for the ages, the message would have had to be more than merely probable. There would have had to be particular details, evidence, to ensure that it could and would be known what the author truly intended.

In actuality, the key to authenticating the meaning stands out in one line, in Act I, scene 5: "Yes, by Saint Patrick, but there is, Horatio, and much offense too." Three times in quick succession the playwright, playing on the word, speaks of offense. Hamlet has spoken, according to Horatio, "wild and whirling words" after his encounter with the Ghost. Hamlet responds:

Hamlet

I am sorry they offend you, heartily;

Yes, faith, heartily.

Horatio

> There's no offense, my lord.

Hamlet

> Yes, by Saint Patrick, but there is, Horatio,
>
> And much offense, too.

> (Act 1, scene 5, 149 – 153)

The author of the play makes clear by the insistent tone of the last line that the repetition is more than a mere play on words. Hamlet unequivocally wants Horatio to know there has been great offense, although he does not yet reveal to him the nature of it.

PART ONE

Parallels and Echoes

The playwright, having directed the reader's attention, early in the play, to Saint Patrick, and thus to his works, establishes a credible foundation for, as well as a key to unlocking, the allegorical interpretation that will be discussed.

The person who reads *Epistola* and is at all familiar with *Hamlet* should quickly recognize themes and other elements of that ancient work that bring the play immediately to mind: poison, madness, flattery, collaboration with a murderer who has killed his "brethren," the public presentation before the evildoers of their grievous offenses.

Certain details, or even individual words, in *Confessio* should cause the reader to take further note: sun, light, anointing, sinking into mire, a three-day sea voyage, hesitating to do something of importance. If the parallels were not intended, the coincidence of these details and others being in both Saint Patrick's works and *Hamlet* would be downright uncanny.

Just as the reference to Saint Patrick is key to understanding the message of the play, Hamlet's statement of what he now must do, having heard the revelations of the Ghost, is the clue to the playwright's mission in writing the play.

At the end of Act I, Hamlet declares:

The time is out of joint. O cursed spite
That ever I was born to set it right!

(Act 1, Scene 5, 210–211)

As will be discussed, the Ghost's command to "revenge," in reality, to vindicate, to set things right, can readily be seen, with the play's allusions to the Jesuits and to the Church militant (Ecclesia militans), as representing the mission of the Counter-Reformation.

In addition, those elements of the play that seem odd, out of place, inconsistent with Hamlet's character, will be seen to make perfect sense in the context of the allegorical meaning. Chief among these is the Ghost's command to Hamlet to seek revenge, but to "[T]aint not thy mind."

It cannot be emphasized enough that in seeking to understand the playwright's allegorical meaning in *Hamlet*, the reader must remain objective, must adhere to the totality of textual evidence in the play, and must keep in mind the context of the time in which the play was written.

I OFFENSE AGAINST CHRISTIANITY: COROTICUS/HENRY VIII

Most critics explain Hamlet's reference to Saint Patrick as an allusion to a place called Saint Patrick's Purgatory in Ireland. A legend had developed, associated with Saint Patrick, and appearing in written texts by the twelfth century, that pilgrims visiting the site on Station Island in Lough Derg witnessed purgatory.

However, the invoking of Saint Patrick, known as the Apostle of Ireland, should make clear that the author is more likely alluding to an offense against Christianity, against the Church unified, as it had been in the fifth century when Patrick spread the faith in Ireland. Furthermore, crucial to understanding the playwright's invoking Saint Patrick is recognizing how the offense in Patrick's works directly parallels the allegorical meaning of the offense in *Hamlet*.

Saint Patrick wrote *Epistola* in order that his condemnation of Coroticus and his soldiers, for their offense of murdering and selling into slavery the captive Christians, be read before them. The offense of Coroticus is his betrayal of the baptized Christians in Ireland.

Played upon the English stage, *Hamlet,* likewise, portrayed before the Crown its offense. The offense, on the allegorical level, is Henry VIII's betrayal of the faithful in England, cutting them off from Sacred Tradition and from the Apostolic Authority of the Church.

The Ghost has, in Act I, scene 5 of the play, revealed to Hamlet the offense that is the "matter" of the play: Claudius's murder of the King, and his marriage, in less than a month, to the Queen. In less than a month, Henry VIII's marriage to Catherine of Aragon was declared on 23 May 1533 "null and void" ("Wives of Henry VIII") by Thomas Cranmer, Archbishop of Canterbury; Henry's public marriage to Anne Boleyn, performed on 25 January 1533, was declared by Cranmer, on 28 May 1533, to be "good and valid" ("Wives of Henry VIII"), and finally on 1 June 1533, Anne Boleyn was crowned Queen.

Claudius has married his brother's wife, as had Henry VIII, who based his case for an annulment of his marriage to Catherine of Aragon on the Old Testament prohibition against a man taking his brother's wife. Both Hamlet and the Ghost accuse Claudius of an incestuous marriage. With the Act of Supremacy in 1534, Henry wedded to the State the sovereignty of the English Church, a union too close, "incestuous." By making himself head of the Church in England, Henry usurped the authority of the Bishop of Rome, the Pope.

In *Epistola*, Patrick's censure includes those British clergy who "implicitly" (de Paor 178) condoned Coroticus:

> Whence, therefore I beseech most of all, [you] 'holy and HUMBLE
>
> OF HEART',
>
> that it be not permissible to flatter such people,
>
> 'to take food' or drink with them,
>
> nor ought one be obliged to accept their alms . . .

(E 7: 50- 53), (de Paor 283)

The play can be seen as representing, allegorically, different elements of the Church: Gertrude, Hamlet's mother, Holy Mother Church in England, seduced away from orthodoxy; Polonius, chief adviser to the king, the politic clergy who did Henry's bidding; Ophelia, daughter of Polonius, the faithful who dutifully obeyed the English Church; Laertes, son of Polonius, the more worldly, less spiritual laity. Hamlet, Horatio, and Fortinbras together can be seen as representing the author of the play, his mission, and his legacy.

The Ghost, murdered as he slept, even with the "blossoms" of his sin still upon him, represents the Bishop of Rome, the Apostolic Authority of the Church. The Vicar of Christ on earth, the Pope is also a human being, and, thus, except in matters of dogma, can err. The Church, which is both the Mystical Body of Christ and the erring human institution, had slept as the Reformation struck, as had the King when murdered.

In *Confessio,* Saint Patrick recounts how at the age of fifteen, from his father's estate in Britain, he was taken captive by Irish raiders. Held in captivity for six years, Patrick suffered hardship and isolation as he tended sheep on the west coast of Ireland. In his loneliness he prayed, and embraced more deeply and fully the Christianity into which he had been born. After escape and return to Britain, Saint Patrick answered the call to return to Ireland and convert the pagan Irish to Christianity.

To Patrick, therefore, as to the author of the play, the offense of corrupting the faithful is an offense of most grievous proportion. Coroticus not only has murdered the baptized men, but also has sold into slavery the baptized maidens. The spoils Patrick compares to poisoned food served at table. Of Coroticus and his collaborators, Patrick states in *Epistola*: ". . . they offer poison, a / deadly food to their own friends and children. . ." (E 13: 125).

Henry too has committed grievous offense; he has corrupted the Faith, and thus the faithful. He has given to them a poisoned cup to drink. He has spread the poison of heresy; he has "tainted" the faithful.

II CONSECRATED LIFE / GET THEE TO A NUNNERY

Like the allusion to Saint Patrick, Hamlet's telling Ophelia, his beloved, in Act III, scene 1, to get to a nunnery is explained, but not quite fully, by critics. Hamlet's charge to Ophelia to get to a nunnery could be taken as his warning her to protect herself from the corrupt world.

However, in relation to *Epistola*, and especially to *Confessio*, this detail has greater significance. Just as the playwright repeats the word offense, he does so with nunnery, in fact repeating it five times, and in quick succession. By emphasizing the word nunnery, he calls attention to it rather than to the world's corruption.

In both *Epistola* and *Confessio*, the consecrated life figures prominently. In the latter, Patrick writes of the baptized in Ireland, "those who never had a knowledge of God," who were pagan, but who are now called "children of God" (C 41: 61), (de Paor 251). Their faith is such that the "sons and daughters of the petty Irish kings / are seen to be monks and virgins of Christ" (C 41: 62- 63). Of their commitment to living a consecrated life, Patrick states further:

> ... all virgins of God do this even now,
> not with their fathers' consent
> but they even suffer persecutions
> and false reproaches from their own parents,
> and nevertheless their number ever increases ...
>
> (C 42: 73- 77)

In marked contrast, Ophelia has obeyed her father when he commands her to have nothing to do with Hamlet, even after she has defended Hamlet, saying that he speaks with all the "holy vows of heaven." By obeying her father, who fears his daughter will "tender" him a fool by trusting what he calls Hamlet's "unholy suits" (1.3.138), Ophelia, a good and dutiful daughter, has gone against her own beliefs, against what she knows to be true, against Hamlet's holy vows.

Ophelia's obedience to Polonius contrasts sharply with the commitment of the Irish sons and daughters to their faith. In obeying Polonius, servile and flattering to the Crown, Ophelia, allegorically, is in effect obeying the Church in England that, like those British clerics who tacitly condoned Coroticus and may have benefited from his spoils, is politic in acquiescing to the will of Henry VIII. Faithful as Ophelia may be, her obedience is misplaced, not well discerned.

In the fifth century, when Saint Patrick spread Christianity to the pagan Irish, the monastic tradition was not yet well established in the West. In England, under Henry, the monasteries and convents had been destroyed. The nunnery, therefore, represents not a place, but a commitment to belief, a choice to live fully consecrated to the Faith.

Allegorically, in the play then, the nunnery represents the commitment of those who practiced their faith, even when doing so put them at risk. Just as the baptized "sons and daughters" in Ireland faced persecution and reproach, so too the recusant Catholics in Elizabethan England faced fines, prison, or death.

In telling Ophelia to get to a nunnery, Hamlet is telling her to protect herself from the corruption of heresy, to separate from the Church of England, to return to the Faith. When viewed in relation to *Confessio* and *Epistola*, Hamlet's charge to Ophelia can be understood with absolute clarity.

III READ BEFORE ALL THE PEOPLE / THE PLAY WITHIN THE PLAY

I n *Epistola,* Saint Patrick makes fully known his intent in writing this letter to Coroticus and his accomplices. He states in his conclusion:

> I earnestly request that whatever servant of God shall volunteer
>
> to be a bearer of this letter,
>
> that on no account it be stolen,
>
> or hidden by anyone,
>
> but rather that it be read before all the people,
>
> even in the presence of Coroticus himself.

> (E 21: 209- 214)

Saint Patrick goes on to emphasize the gravity of the deed: killing those who are "brethren of the Lord." His further desire is that his letter inspire Coroticus and his collaborators to repent, that they may be restored to their right minds, to reason, to their senses, and be made whole:

> May God inspire them, at some time or another, 'to return to their senses before God',
> so that they may repent [however] late of such a heinous deed,
> the murder of the brethren of the Lord,
> and that they may release *the baptized* captive women whom they previously seized,
> that they may thus deserve to live for God
> and be made whole
> *here and for eternity*
> Peace to the Father and to the Son and to the Holy Spirit. Amen.
>
> (E 21: 215– 222)

Likewise, "The Murder of Gonzago," the play within the play, reenacts before Claudius his offense, the murder of his brother and marriage to the Queen. More significantly, *Hamlet*, performed on the London stage, sets before the Crown its own offense, Henry VIII making himself head of the Church in England, and with the Act of Supremacy in 1534, wedding Church to State.

Hamlet has planned the play within the play to portray before the King the grievousness of his deed. Hamlet states in his soliloquy, in Act II, scene 2, his intent: "The play's

the thing / Wherein I'll catch the conscience of the King"
(2.2.633-634).

IV ESTRANGED / EXCOMMUNICATED

In *Epistola*, Saint Patrick declares Coroticus and his collaborators "estranged" from God. In the play, the deaths of Rosencrantz and Guildenstern, and Claudius, symbolically represent their estrangement from communion with the Church, in other words, their excommunication. In fact, in 1538, Henry VIII was excommunicated by Pope Paul III. In the act of spying for the King, Polonius, allegorically in cooperation with heresy, has estranged himself from communion with the Church.

Saint Patrick says of those "whom the devil has gravely ensnared":

> Wherefore let every *God*-fearing person learn
> that *they are estranged from me*
> and from *Christ my God,*
> '*for whom I am an ambassador*'.

(E 5: 32-35)

Hamlet acts with equal authority when he seals Rosencrantz's and Guildenstern's death warrants with his father's signet. Hamlet's dispatching of Claudius with the poisoned cup, the poison that Claudius himself has spread, represents, on the allegorical level, Henry VIII's excommunication, his being cut off by the poison of his own heresy; he is out of communion with the Church. Just as Claudius killed the King and usurped his authority, Henry had usurped the authority of the Bishop of Rome, the Pope.

King Hamlet is allegorically that Papal authority, the Apostolic Authority of the Church passed from Saint Peter to each of his successors, who were elected largely by clergy and laity, and beginning in 1274, by papal conclave of the College of Cardinals. It is with that same authority, symbolized by the signet, that Prince Hamlet cuts off those who have committed grave offense against the Church. As Hamlet states in Act 5, scene 2, Claudius has come between "th' election" and his, Hamlet's, "hopes" (5.2.73). In other words, Hamlet is literally the successor to the King, but is, allegorically, to have been the next successor of Peter.

In *Epistola*, Saint Patrick urges Coroticus, who is estranged, to repent and be redeemed, to be made whole "here and for eternity." The playwright's purpose in *Hamlet* is to instruct the English to return to the Faith, that they, likewise, may return to their senses, be made whole.

The playwright wants to make known, through the medium of the play, the need for vindication: to set things right. As it was supposed that the Ghost would communicate in Latin, his command to Hamlet to revenge his murder should be more associated with the Latin "vindicare," from which "revenge" is derived, than with the ancient code of "an eye for an eye."

That Hamlet seems to understand that he is commanded to vindicate, to justify, to show what is true, is made clear when he professes that "with wings as swift / As meditation or the thoughts of love" (1.5.35-36), he will "sweep" to his revenge. Allegorically, the Ghost's command to revenge his murder is thus obligating Hamlet not to commit bloody murder, but, rather, to defend the Faith, to set things right.

Hamlet's being both untroubled and absolutely remorseless for those deaths for which he is intentionally responsible, seems, with Hamlet's finely tuned conscience, wholly out of character. Even for his killing of Polonius, Hamlet is at first unrepentant.

His state of mind makes perfect sense, however, if the deaths, as well as Hamlet's seemingly unkind treatment of Polonius, are seen, allegorically, as representing excommunication, or, in other words, defense of the Faith. Seen in relation to Saint Patrick's *Epistola,* Hamlet's treatment of Polonius, which otherwise can be most difficult to comprehend and explain, becomes understandable.

Polonius is the father of Hamlet's beloved. He is, as well, a foolish old man, whose faults make him appear more vulnerable and human than evil; he is tedious, long-winded, servile, and self-serving. He can, however, admit when he thinks he is wrong, as he does when Ophelia describes

Hamlet's strange appearance and behavior when Hamlet unexpectedly appeared before her. Forgetful, Polonius must be reminded of his command that Ophelia avoid Hamlet. Truly regretful, however, Polonius states, in Act II, scene 1, "That hath made him mad. / I am sorry that with better heed and judgment / I had not coted him" (2.1.123-125).

Hamlet's mockery of Polonius, and his eventual killing of him when Hamlet mistakes Polonius for Claudius behind an arras in Gertrude's chamber, seem most unlike "sterling" Hamlet largely because he shows no remorse, at least not until later in the play. In Act 2, scene 2, in an aside, and in a most dismissive tone, Hamlet calls Polonius a "tedious" old fool (2.2.237). Yet, the reader has already witnessed Polonius rather pathetically make a fool of himself by his long-winded effort to tell Claudius and Gertrude that he has discovered the cause of Hamlet's lunacy. Later, when Hamlet strikes through the curtain and discovers that it is Polonius, not Claudius, that he has killed, he quickly shifts blame for the murder onto the dead Polonius, even insulting him in the process:

> Thou wretched, rash, intruding fool, farewell.
> I took thee for thy better. Take thy fortune.
> Thou find'st to be too busy is some danger.
>
> (Act 3, scene 4, 38 – 40)

Hamlet displays even more blatant lack of remorse when he secretly arranges that the servile and spying Rosencrantz and Guildenstern be put to death immediately upon their arrival in England, no shriving time allowed. Just as Claudius had murdered Hamlet's father as he slept, with the "blossoms" of his sin still upon him, no "reck'ning made" (1.5.85), Rosencrantz and Guildenstern, as did Polonius, die unshriven, caught in the trap of heresy. Yet, when Hamlet reveals to Horatio his having sent Rosencrantz and Guildenstern to their deaths, he states, in Act V, scene 2, "They are not near my conscience" (5.2.65).

Hamlet's forcing the poisoned wine down the throat of Claudius, justified though it may seem, is, nonetheless, deliberate murder, and committed as Hamlet seems to ridicule the King:

> Here, thou incestuous, (murd'rous,) damned Dane,
> Drink off this potion. Is (thy union) here?
>
> (Act 5, scene 2, 356 – 357)

On the literal level, Hamlet is referring to the poisoned pearl which Claudius has placed in the cup of wine, having stated:

> If Hamlet give the first or second hit…
>
> (Act 5, scene 2, 287)

> The King shall drink to Hamlet's better breath,
> And in the cup an (union) shall he throw,
> Richer than that which four successive kings …
>
> (Act 5, scene 2, 290 – 292)

Also, "union" is a play on words, referring to Claudius's marriage to Gertrude.

Allegorically, however, the union is Henry VIII's joining together of Church and State under his authority. Polonius, and Rosencrantz and Guildenstern, represent those, including those clergy, who benefited from cooperating with Henry in breaking from the Church. Their offense is against the faithful in England, just as Coroticus's offense is against the faithful in Ireland. Coroticus and his cohort have offended by murdering and holding captive; the English crown and its collaborators have offended by spreading the venom of heresy, by holding souls captive. They are thus, like Coroticus, estranged, out of communion with the Church, until which time they become reconciled.

Saint Patrick, as an ambassador of God, has acted with authority in declaring those whom the devil has gravely ensnared to be estranged. Likewise, Hamlet, allegorically, acting with the authority of the Church, has, by his actions, declared Henry and those who collaborated with him to be estranged.

As Saint Patrick states in *Epistola*:

> For it is written: 'Not only those who commit evil deeds,
> but also those who agree with them are to be condemned.'

> (E 14: 138– 139)

V LIGHT AMONG THE PAGANS / GIVE ME SOME LIGHT

Light is central to both *Hamlet* and to Saint Patrick's *Confessio*. At almost the very middle of the play, after the play within the play, Claudius, having seen his offense enacted before him, cries, "Give me some light" (3.2.295). Claudius calls for light in order to be saved from his own darkness. As Marie B. de Paor, PBVM (Sr. Declan), in *PATRICK The Pilgrim Apostle of Ireland*, points out (de Paor 272), in Part IV of *Confessio* Patrick echoes both Acts 13 and Isaiah 49: "... 'I have placed you as a light among the pagans, / so that you may bring salvation to the ends of the earth' ..." (C 38: 14- 15). In Part V, knowledge of the "true sun, Christ" (C 60: 37) is contrasted to pagan adoration of the sun.

Hamlet also contains reference to the sun in an exchange between Hamlet and Claudius in Act 1, scene 2.

King

    But now, my cousin Hamlet and my son –

Hamlet

    A little more than kin and less than kind.

King

    How is it that the clouds still hang on you?

Hamlet

    Not so, my lord; I am too much in the sun.

                      (Act 1, scene 2, 66 – 69)

Quick-witted Hamlet thus insults Claudius who, though his uncle, is now, as a result of Claudius's marriage to the Queen less than a month after King Hamlet's death, also his father. Allegorically, Hamlet can be seen as declaring that he is amidst pagans, sun worshippers, heretics, cut off from the Faith.

As will be discussed, the play has clear connection to the Society of Jesus and to *The Spiritual Exercises of Saint Ignatius*. Therefore, the sun reference may be, also, an allusion to the Seal of the Society of Jesus, which has a Christogram, a cross, and three nails, surrounded by a sunburst.

VI REJOICING GREATLY
/ FRIGHTED WITH
FALSE FIRE

S aint Patrick recounts, in Part II of *Confessio*, several mystical experiences, dreams, or visions. In a dream, Satan puts Patrick "*to the test*," falling upon him "*like a huge rock*" and leaving him with "*no power*" over his limbs (C 20: 85). Patrick calls upon Elijah with all his "might," and states that "*lo, the splendour of his sun [helios] fell on me, / and immediately freed me of all oppressiveness ...*" (C 20: 89-90). In another, what he calls a "vision of the night" (C 23: 116), Patrick hears the Voice of the Irish calling him back to Ireland, to walk once more among them. It is then revealed to Patrick in a dream that the Voice of Christ is speaking within him, calling him to the mission to Ireland (de Paor 97). In a further mystical experience, Patrick is made aware that the Spirit is praying within him.

From the dream of Christ speaking within him, Patrick states that he was "awakened rejoicing greatly" (C 24: 141).

As Marie B. de Paor, PBVM, (Sr. Declan), again in *PATRICK The Pilgrim Apostle of Ireland*, states:

> The immediate effect of this experience was that Patrick woke up full of the Spirit of Joy, the sure sign of the Presence of God, that same Spirit who pervades and illuminates his entire *Confessio.*
>
> (dePaor 97)

With equal joy, Hamlet has witnessed Claudius's expression of guilt, his calling for light, after Claudius sees his own crime enacted before him in the play within the play. Saint Patrick rejoices at the knowledge of God's presence within him. Hamlet rejoices at the knowledge of which he can now be certain, that the Ghost is honest, that the spirit he has seen is not from the devil. He cries to Claudius, "What, frighted with false fire?" (3.2.292), and declares to Horatio:

> O good Horatio, I'll take the ghost's word for
> a thousand pound. Didst perceive?
>
> (Act 3, scene 2, 312 - 313)

Both Patrick and Hamlet rejoice at a sign confirming what they believe to be true. Claudius, calling for light, seems briefly, in that moment, to seek the antidote to his own evil, that same comfort of the Spirit, that was for Saint Patrick, a sign of the Presence of God.

VII ANOINTED WITH CHRISM / I'LL ANOINT MY SWORD

In *Epistola*, Saint Patrick describes the newly baptized Irish Christians caught in Coroticus's raid. Not only do they wear the white robes signifying their new lives in Christ, but, also, they still have on their foreheads the chrism, or holy oil, with which they were anointed when confirmed. In the early Church, the sacraments of Baptism, Confirmation, and Eucharist were administered on the same occasion, as part of the Christian's initiation into the Church. The chrism signified the Christian's being sealed with the Holy Spirit.

In Act IV of *Hamlet*, the playwright likewise alludes, in quick succession, to three sacraments: Extreme Unction (Anointing of the Sick), the Eucharist, and Baptism. The allegorical meaning derived from these allusions is that the Church in England, tainted by heresy, offered the newly baptized an initiation not into the sacramental life of the Church, but rather into a corruption of the Church, devoid of sacramental grace.

In *Epistola*, Saint Patrick says of the newly baptized Christians:

> On the day following that on which *the newly baptized* in white
> clothing were anointed with chrism,
> it was still shining on their foreheads while they were cruelly
> slaughtered and slain with the sword …

(E 3: 20- 21)

In contrast to the holy oil used to anoint the Irish Christians in their new life in the Spirit, the grieving Laertes, plans, in Act 4, scene 7, to anoint his sword with poison, conspiring with, and manipulated by Claudius, to avenge the death of Polonius, his father, by killing Hamlet:

King

> …what would you undertake
> To show yourself indeed your father's son
> More than in words?

Laertes

> To cut his throat i' th' church.

(Act 4, scene 7, 141 - 144)

King

> …you may choose
> A sword unbated, and in a (pass) of practice
> Requite him for your father.

Laertes

> I will do 't,
> And for (that) purpose I'll anoint my sword.
> I bought an unction of a mountebank
> So mortal that, but dip a knife in it …
>
> (Act 4 scene 7, 156 – 162)

Clearly, the diction in this passage suggests that the playwright is alluding to the sacrament of Extreme Unction, the anointing of the sick and dying. The person receiving the sacrament was anointed with holy oil, chrism, for spiritual comfort and benefit.

Yet, in Article 25 of the Thirty-nine Articles of 1571, the Church of England considered Extreme Unction to be not a sacrament, but a rite, a "corrupted" imitation "of the Apostles" ("Thirty-nine Articles").

However, as the Council of Trent had declared in 1551:

ON THE SACRAMENT OF EXTREME UNCTION

CANON I. - If any one saith, that Extreme Unction is not truly and properly a sacrament, instituted by Christ our Lord, and promulgated by the blessed apostle James; but is only a rite received from the Fathers, or a human figment; let him be anathema.

Session the Fourteenth, on the twenty-fifth of November MDLI

("The Council of Trent")

Laertes and Claudius, plotting to revenge with an "anointed" sword, together have symbolically corrupted the rite, which in turn was a corruption of the sacrament. Rather than being an aid to physical or spiritual healing, Laertes's anointing of his sword, an instrument of death and revenge, further spreads, allegorically, the poison of heresy.

If Hamlet is but scratched by the poisoned sword, he will die; in contrast, the baptized and confirmed Christian has gained new life in the Spirit. The anointing in *Hamlet* echoes the anointing in *Epistola*, but, rather than being a direct parallel, is a perversion of it, and is thus symbolic of heresy spread in England.

Claudius devises a backup plan, a chalice of poisoned wine, if the proposed duel between Laertes and Hamlet should fail:

> And that he calls for drink, I'll have prepared
>> him
> A chalice for the nonce, whereon but sipping,
> If he by chance escape your venomed stuck,
> Our purpose may hold there. - But stay, what
>> noise?

> (Act 4, Scene 7, 181 - 186)

Gertrude enters at that moment to announce that Ophelia, Laertes's sister, has drowned, pulled to her "muddy" death by her garments "heavy with their drink" (4.7.206).

"Too much of water hast thou, poor Ophelia," Laertes says (4.7.211).

The playwright thus has alluded to three sacraments: Extreme Unction, the Eucharist, and Baptism. The water, symbolizing Baptism, into which Ophelia falls, is muddied, as is the English Church, into which the baptized enter, muddied by heresy. Just as the playwright's treatment of Extreme Unction is a perversion of the sacrament, his treatment of the Eucharist is as well. The chalice is a cup of poisoned wine, not the Blood of Christ, and the unction is poison, not sacred chrism. The baptized will become tainted, muddied, by the Church in England, initiated not into new life in the Spirit, but rather into spiritual error, the mire of heresy.

The allusion to three sacraments in quick succession echoes *Epistola:* the Irish Christians, newly received into the Church through Baptism, Confirmation, and the Eucharist, only to be "cruelly slaughtered and slain with the sword..." (E 3: 21). Just as Coroticus had "stained his own hands with the blood of the children of God" (E 9: 77), Claudius, himself tainted, perverted, by the poison he spreads, represents Henry who, by spreading heresy, put the souls of the English faithful in peril.

VIII   DEEP MIRE / MUDDY DEATH

The playwright's portrayal of Ophelia's death in *Hamlet*, though in stark contrast, echoes Saint Patrick's *Confessio*, which, in turn, alludes to Psalm 69. Ophelia, as if incapable of saving herself, sinks into the water, pulled to a muddy death. The Psalmist in Psalm 69 prays that the Lord, in his mercy, rescue him from the watery depths, from sinking into the mire. Saint Patrick declares that he was rescued from the deep mire by God in his mercy.

Saint Patrick says of himself:

> ...'I do *know* most surely', that, indeed
> 'BEFORE I WAS HUMBLED'
> I was like a stone lying in 'deep mire',
> and he 'who is mighty' came
> and 'in his mercy' lifted me up ...

> (C 12: 46– 50)

Gertrude says of Ophelia:

> Her clothes spread wide,
> And mermaid-like awhile they bore her up,
> Which time she chanted snatches of old lauds,
> As one incapable of her own distress
> Or like a creature native and endued
> Unto that element. But long it could not be
> Till that her garments, heavy with their drink,
> Pulled the poor wretch from her melodious lay
> To muddy death.

(Act 4, scene 7, 200 – 208)

As Sr. Declan points out in *PATRICK The Pilgrim Apostle of Ireland* (de Paor 268), Patrick echoes The Psalmist in Psalm 69:

> But I pray to you, O Lord,
> > for the time of your favor, O God!
> In your great kindness answer me
> > with your constant help.
> Rescue me out of the mire; may I not
> > sink!
> may I be rescued from my foes,
> and from the watery depths.

(Ps 69, 14 – 15)

> Answer me, O Lord, for bounteous is
>> your kindness;
>> in your great mercy turn toward me.

(Ps 69, 17)

Unlike Saint Patrick and the Psalmist, both rescued by God's mercy, Ophelia is not saved from her muddy death. The Psalmist prays that he may not sink; Ophelia, floating mermaid-like, chants snatches of old lauds.

It is significant that Ophelia is chanting only snatches, fragments, of old lauds, in other words, the remains of the old Faith. Lauds is part of the Liturgy of Hours, the Divine Office. The Book of Common Prayer of 1549 had reduced the canonical hours (Matins, Lauds, Prime, Terce, Sext, Nones, Vespers, Compline), the fixed times for daily prayer, from eight to two: Morning Prayers and Evening Prayers. In chanting snatches of old lauds, Ophelia is, in effect, unable to complete the ancient prayer in praise of God.

Ophelia's prayer is thus diminished, just as the rites that are Ophelia's funeral are "maimed" (5.1.226). The Gravedigger debates the question of her death, and why she is to be buried in Christian burial, if she "willfully" sought her own "salvation" (5.1.2). He says that such burial cannot be, unless she had drowned in her own defense. He argues further that if she drowned knowingly, it required an act; she had to perform the act, and thus she "drowned herself wittingly" (5.1.13).

The Gravedigger's debate, accentuating Ophelia's action, is suggestive of the Reformist doctrine of sola fide, justification by faith alone. In contrast to what the Church had taught, that justification, forgiveness, is by faith and works, the Church of England taught, as had Luther, that justification is by faith alone. Thus, the Gravedigger, by emphasizing Ophelia's action, appears not to accept the Reformist doctrine.

Easily overlooked is the Gravedigger's song, which seems hardly to make any sense. Its significance becomes apparent, though, when recognized that it alludes to a recusant Catholic, Henry Vaux, who, along with members of his family, was instrumental in smuggling priests into England. The Gravedigger's song mimics a poem, "The Aged Lover Renounceth Love" (Shakespeare 242), by Thomas Vaux, Second Baron Vaux of Harrowden. The poem was published in Tottel's *Miscellaney* in 1557. Thomas Vaux's grandson was Henry Vaux.

It is odd, and therefore noteworthy, that the Gravedigger uses the word "salvation" when speaking of Ophelia's seemingly willful drowning. If willed, then her action would appear more an effort to escape, perhaps from her grief. If her death is the result of madness, she would be considered incapable of wittingly seeking "her own salvation."

In stark contrast to the clarity voiced by Saint Patrick and the Psalmist, that God's mercy is what saves, the circumstances of Ophelia's death are ambiguous. Is she responsible for her own death? Is she seeking escape or salvation? Does she gain salvation? The accrual of allusions, to Saint Patrick, Psalm 69, the canonical hours, Henry Vaux, all point to "salvation" being intended in a spiritual, rather than a psychological, sense.

Furthermore, in contrast to the metaphoric "unweeded garden" (1.2.139) that Denmark has become, Ophelia is hanging garlands of "crowflowers, nettles, daisies, and long purples" (4.7.193) when she falls into the brook. Is she attempting to restore the metaphoric "garden," the Church unified, in which King Hamlet slept when Claudius poisoned him?

Ophelia is pulled down by her garments "heavy with their drink" (4.7.206). This image, following closely upon the image of the poisoned chalice proposed by Claudius to Laertes, might suggest that the "drink" is not the water of the brook, but is, allegorically, the wine that, poisoned by heresy, would not, according to recusant Catholics, provide spiritual benefit. Spreading flowers, and chanting lauds, is Ophelia attempting to reclaim the old Faith? Is she, however, so submerged in the mire, in the poison of heresy, bereft of sacramental grace, that she cannot save herself from sinking?

Perhaps the playwright wants us ultimately to understand that we cannot usurp the authority that is God's alone, that we cannot, nor should we think ourselves capable of, discerning what judgment awaits Ophelia. We can only wonder if Ophelia, "clamb'ring" precariously on the branch of the willow, hanging metaphorically, as it were, between hope of salvation and fear of damnation, is, in the end, saved. Might the playwright's allusions to Saint Patrick and the Psalmist lead us to hope that Ophelia too is saved by God's mercy?

IX BE MADE WHOLE / MADNESS

In *Epistola*, Saint Patrick hopes to inspire Coroticus to return to his senses, to be made whole, in other words, to return to reason, to regain right judgment, a sense of what is true. In the play, Ophelia has gone mad, has lost her senses. The most obvious cause of her madness would seem to be grief over her father's death. Laertes and Gertrude also behave irrationally, Laertes in an angry passion, and Gertrude by allowing her passions to rule her judgment. Hamlet, too, must exert his will at times to control his passions.

Both Coroticus and Ophelia have lost right judgment of what is true and good. Coroticus has valued the "spoils" more than the lives of his captives. Ophelia, in obeying her father, has gone against what she knows to be true: Hamlet's holy vows. She has complied with what she knows to be false: Polonius's misjudgment of Hamlet. Allegorically, Ophelia has obeyed what she knows to be heretical.

Coroticus's lost sense of what is right produces death and suffering. Ophelia's allegiance to what is false, symbolized by her grief over Polonius's death, leads Ophelia into madness, into a tainted reality, away from sound judgment.

In *Epistola*, Saint Patrick speaks of mourning for the captured Christians:

> *Therefore* the Church *'bewails and laments*
> *her own sons' and daughters*
> *whom so far the sword has not yet killed,*
> but who are banished and deported to distant lands ...

(E 15: 148- 151)

Therefore I shall cry aloud in sadness and grief:

O most beautiful and *most beloved brethren and children 'whom I have*
   begotten in Christ' ...

(E 16: 156– 157)

> Therefore I grieve for you
> I grieve, my dearest ones ...

(E 17: 168– 169)

In Act 4, scene 5 of the play, Ophelia sings of her grief. She seems almost to echo Patrick's lament for his fellow Christians:

> *And will he not come again?*
> *And will he not come again?*
> *No, no, he is dead.*
> *Go to thy deathbed.*
> *He never will come again.*
>
> *His beard was as white as snow,*
> *(All) flaxen was his poll.*
> *He is gone, he is gone,*
> *And we cast away moan.*
> *God 'a mercy on his soul.*

And of all Christians' souls, (I pray God.) God be wi' you.

(Act 4, scene 5, 213 – 224)

In the same scene, Ophelia sings rather crude ditties, representing how much she has become tainted, how far she is from her good judgment. The poison of heresy has spread, both affecting and infecting not only Ophelia, but also the whole kingdom. Claudius himself attributes the change in Ophelia to the "poison of deep grief" (4.5.80). He refers also to "the people muddied" (4.5.86). Ophelia sinks into the mire, perhaps never regaining her senses. The poison of heresy has driven her from what is right and true; it has made her mad.

Saint Patrick provides the antidote to the poison:

> May God inspire them, at some time or another, 'to return to
>   their senses before God',
> so that they may repent [however] late of such a heinous deed ...

(E 21: 215– 216)

> . . . that they may thus deserve to live for God
> and be made whole . . .

(E 21: 219- 220)

Both Gertrude, in Act 3, scene 4, and Laertes, in Act 5, scene 2, do repent. Gertrude, weak-willed and seduced by the King, says to Hamlet:

> O Hamlet, speak no more!
> Thou turn'st my eyes into my (very) soul,
> And there I see such black and (grained) spots
> As will (not) leave their tinct.

(Act 3, scene 4, 99 - 102)

Laertes, stuck with his own poisoned sword, and after Claudius has been forced to drink the poison, declares to Hamlet:

He is justly served.

It is a poison tempered by himself.

Exchange forgiveness with me, noble Hamlet.

Mine and my father's death come not upon thee,

Nor thine on me.

(Act 5, scene 2, 359 - 363)

Both Laertes and Gertrude have exhibited loss of reason. Laertes's fury at Hamlet for the killing of his father has impaired his ability to think rationally. He fails to recognize Claudius's duplicity when Claudius claims he could not publicly charge Hamlet with the murder because of his great love for Gertrude, and then immediately proceeds to plot Hamlet's death. Hamlet questions Gertrude about how, if her senses had not been "apoplexed" (3.4.83), she could have replaced the dead King with the likes of Claudius.

Both characters, finally having recognized the treachery and deception of Claudius, confess to their own evil, and are remorseful. Claudius's treachery, the poison he spreads, is symbolically heresy that, like the poison poured into the King's ear, has spread "swift as quicksilver" (1.5.73). Although both Gertrude and Laertes die, affected by that poison, they die repentant and in a state of grace. Hamlet says to Gertrude, "And, when you are desirous to be blest, / I'll blessing beg of you" (3.4.192-193). Having exchanged forgiveness with him before Laertes dies, Hamlet about to die himself, prays that heaven make Laertes free of his, Hamlet's, death.

Both Laertes and Gertrude have returned to their senses. They are absolved of their sins, made whole. Hamlet, during his encounter with his mother, is reminded by the Ghost of his command. Urged by the Ghost to step between Gertrude and her fighting soul, Hamlet turns from his sharp rebuke of Gertrude to showing concern, asking how it is with her. Hamlet, in a rage of passion, has regained control of his senses.

He is made further whole when he turns his attention to the dead Polonius, saying:

> For this same lord
> I do repent; but heaven hath pleased it so
> To punish me with this and this with me,
> That I must be their scourge and minister.
> I will bestow him and will answer well
> The death I gave him.
>
> (Act 3, scene 4, 193 – 198)

As he who, in effect, would have been elected, Hamlet represents the Papal authority, the Church that must both minister to the faithful, and prevent the spread of that which is not orthodox. However, the Church had erred. It had failed to reform. While the Church slept, the poison of heresy had spread.

Hamlet had erred; he had acted rashly in striking through the curtain. By mistake, he had killed the foolish old man. Returned to his senses, he repents.

Is Ophelia, in the end, made whole? Whether or not she dies still mired in heresy, or whether, in her chanting old lauds, she has wits enough to atone and seek mercy, is to our too human minds as muddied as the water into which Ophelia tragically sinks.

Claudius recognizes his sin, seeks to repent, but is unwilling to make amends: he will not give up the crown and the Queen. Claudius dies by his own poison.

Claudius, the "serpent" (1.5.46) who now wears his brother's crown, is, allegorically, Henry VIII who, by usurping the authority of the Church, had attempted, like Satan, the serpent in the garden, to make his will equal to God's. The poison of his own heresy had infected his reason, his right judgment.

X CONVERSION:
PATRICK / HORATIO

Both Saint Patrick and Horatio experience conversion. During his captivity, Patrick converted from a state of youthful ignorance to a state of greater wisdom in which his heart was opened to God. By the end of Act 1, Horatio too, at least in part, will have undergone conversion, from skeptic to believer in the appearance of the Ghost of the dead King.

In *Confessio*, Saint Patrick writes of his conversion during his captivity in Ireland:

> And THERE 'the Lord opened my heart to an awareness of my unbelief'
> so that, perhaps, *I might* at last *remember my sins*,
> and that 'I might turn with all my heart to the Lord my God,'
> who *'turned his gaze round on MY LOWLINESS'*
> and *had mercy on my youth and IGNORANCE*
> and *kept watch over* me before I knew him

and before I was wise or could distinguish between good

and evil ...

(C 2: 20- 26)

At the beginning of the play, Horatio, a friend of Prince Hamlet's, accompanies Marcellus on the watch. A ghost has appeared twice already at precisely one hour past midnight. As a scholar, Horatio, newly returned from Wittenberg, knows Latin; thus, it is believed that he would be able to communicate with the Ghost.

Horatio, at first a skeptic, assumes the Ghost will not appear. However, in the same "fair and warlike form" as the "majesty of buried Denmark," the Ghost comes again. Harrowed with "fear and wonder," trembling and pale, Horatio states that he would not have believed without "the sensible and true avouch / Of mine own eyes" (1.1.67-68). Although the Ghost has not spoken, Horatio predicts, "This bodes some strange eruption to our state" (1.1.80).

The Ghost's appearance with "martial stalk" leads Marcellus to question Denmark's war preparations. Young Prince Fortinbras of Norway, Horatio has heard whispered, of "unimproved mettle hot and full" (1.1.108), seeks to recover "by strong hand" lands lost by his father to the dead King Hamlet, or as Horatio says, "... our valiant Hamlet / (For so this side of our known world esteemed him) ..." (1.1.96-97).

Contemplating the Ghost as "prologue to the omen coming on" (1.1.135), Horatio describes how in Rome, the night before Julius Caesar was assassinated, "... the sheeted dead / Did squeak and gibber in the Roman streets ..." (1.1.127-128). The Ghost reappears, and though Horatio implores that it speak if "there be any good thing to be done / That may to thee do ease and grace to me" (1.1.142-143), the cock crows and again the Ghost departs.

Marcellus recounts that "some" say how just before the Savior's birth is celebrated, the cock "singeth all night long," and that then "no spirit dare stir abroad ... So hallowed and so gracious is that time." "So have I heard and do in part believe it" (1.1.180), Horatio replies. Having doubted the Ghost at first, Horatio proposes that Prince Hamlet be informed of the Ghost's appearance, for, as he says, "... upon my life, / This spirit, dumb to us, will speak to him" (1.1.185-186). The skeptic, more than "in part," now believes.

XI CONVERSIONS AT SEA: SAINT PATRICK (PAGANS) / HAMLET (PIRATES)

Both Saint Patrick, in *Confessio,* and Hamlet tell of a three- day sea voyage. Both tell of having converted those who sailed the ships.

After six years in captivity, Saint Patrick heard a voice in a dream say that soon he would return to his own country. A short time later, he heard another voice saying that his ship was ready. Patrick tells of how, after a journey of perhaps two hundred miles, he reached the ship. After three days, the ship reached land. For twenty-eight days on land, Patrick and the sailors, who were pagan, found no food, and were overcome by hunger.

As Saint Patrick recounts:

... and on the next day the captain began to say to me:
'How is this, Christian?
You say your God is great and all-powerful?
Why then can you not PRAY for us?

(C 19: 55– 58)

But *I said* to them with confidence:
"'Be converted' in faith 'with all your heart to the Lord *my*
    God ...'"

(C 19: 61– 62)

Saint Patrick goes on to state that a herd of pigs soon appeared on the road before them, and the sailors "rendered the highest thanks to God." Saint Patrick states that he became "*honourable in their eyes*" (C 19: 74).

Sent by Claudius to England, in the company of Rosencrantz and Guildenstern, after the killing of Polonius, Hamlet is aboard ship, and attacked by pirates.

Horatio reads Hamlet's account in a letter:

Ere we were two days
old at sea, a pirate of very warlike appointment gave
us chase. Finding ourselves too slow of sail, we put on
a compelled valor, and in the grapple I boarded them.
On the instant, they got clear of our ship; so I alone
became their prisoner. They have dealt with me like

thieves of mercy, but they knew what they did: I am to
do a (good) turn for them.

(Act 4, scene 6, 15 – 22)

The sailors have brought Hamlet back to Denmark.
Hamlet, in the letter, tells Horatio that these "good fellows"
will bring Horatio to where he is.

Hamlet's sea journey of a day and part of a day going,
and the same in returning, in other words, three days, parallels Saint Patrick's sea voyage of three days. Patrick's conversion of the pagan sailors into believing in God's having
provided them with food is mirrored by Hamlet's trans-
forming, with promise of reward, the warlike pirates into
agents of mercy.

The sailors who had thanked God also offered to Patrick a taste of wild honey, one of them informing him that
it was a pagan sacrifice. Patrick did not taste the honey.
Likewise, the pirates who have behaved so mercifully to
Hamlet, are recognized by Hamlet still to be thieves. The
pagans who offered thanks, as well as the thieves who show
mercy, are like the early Christians who, though converted,
still preserved remnants of pagan practice.

In contrast to the newly converted, (the sailors who
believed and were thankful, and the thieves who, believing in a promised reward, acted with mercy), are Henry
VIII and Coroticus. Henry, thankless, squandered the truth
passed down with authority from the Apostles. Coroticus
plundered and murdered without mercy.

The pagan Irish were unenlightened, were without knowledge of God. The English faithful practiced a corrupted faith: the remnants of the old Faith, tainted by heresy, a perversion of truth.

Saint Patrick, Apostle of the Irish, answered a call to convert, to enlighten by way of truth. The playwright, apostle of the English, answered a call to convert those in England away from heresy and back to the Faith.

XII IRELAND: DENMARK

Might the settting of the play, Denmark, represent, allegorically, what Saint Patrick termed "the limit beyond which nobody dwells"? As Sr. Declan points out in *PATRICK The Pilgrim Apostle of Ireland*, "Ireland, the land of Patrick's captivity, was outside the confines of the Roman Empire" (de Paor 30).

Sr. Declan states further:

> Since his father was a decurion, a deacon, and the owner of an estate
>
> we conclude that Patrick belonged to the Romanised British nobility
>
> who had been Christians for at least three generations. He always
>
> remained proud of his Roman citizenship, which was, for him,
>
> synonymous with being a Christian (de Paor 28).

Historically, Denmark, too, had been considered outside the limits of the Roman Empire. Might Denmark under Claudius allegorically represent England under Henry VIII?

Is the playwright thus drawing a parallel between Ireland, pagan in the time of Saint Patrick, and England, unorthodox in its belief, having broken with Rome in the Reformation?

XIII THE TRINITY: SAINT PATRICK / HAMLET

Fundamental to *Confessio* is Saint Patrick's devotion to the Trinity: Father, Son, Holy Spirit. Saint Patrick states:

> And so, 'according to the measure of the faith' of the
> 	Trinity it is my duty,
> *without fear of the censure [I may incur],*
> *to make known 'THE GIFT OF GOD'*
> and [his] 'eternal consolation';
> *without fear*
> faithfully *to expound everywhere the name of God* ...
>
> 			(C 14: 71– 76)

As Maire B. de Paor (Sister Declan), PBVM, affirms: "In the face of injustice Patrick's gaze is ever fixed on the Blessed Trinity and the eternal reward of patient endurance" (de Paor 55).

It is interesting to note that in *Hamlet*, the playwright has devised much in triplicate: Prince Hamlet, Fortinbras, Laertes, three sons with fathers killed; three soldiers, Francisco, Bernardo, Marcellus, on watch at the beginning of the play; Hamlet, Horatio, Fortinbras who, by the end of the play, have the same mission, to restore legitimate authority to Denmark.

XIV BIBLICAL ALLUSIONS: SAINT PATRICK / HAMLET

S aint Patrick's *Confessio* and *Epistola* contain an abundance of Biblical allusions. *Hamlet* contains a significant number of Biblical allusions as well, and, in fact, the playwright echoes very meaningfully some of those allusions in Patrick's work.

Sr. Declan includes the full texts of both *Confessio* and *Epistola* in *PATRICK The Pilgrim Apostle of Ireland.* After each, she lists the many Biblical references that correspond to the work.

For instance, Sr. Declan relates Matthew 7 to Patrick's likening Coroticus to a ravenous wolf. Patrick states in Epistola:

'Rapacious wolves' have swallowed up the flock of the Lord,
which was indeed growing excellently in Ireland with the
greatest loving care.

(E 12: 114- 115)

Saint Patrick's charge against Coroticus clearly echoes Matthew 7:

> Be on your guard against false prophets, who come to you in
> sheep's clothing but underneath are wolves on the prowl. You will
> know them by their deeds.
>
> (Mt 7, 15-16)

Patrick further accuses Coroticus:

> … *you* rather kill and *sell them to a remote pagan people* ignorant of
> God;
> *you are handing over*, as it were, 'the members of Christ' into a
> brothel.
> What hope in God have you,
> or anyone who concurs with you?
> or who converses with you in words of flattery?
>
> (E 14: 132– 136)

Patrick's reference to the brothel is echoed in *Hamlet* by Claudius when he states:

> The harlot's cheek beautied with plast'ring art
> Is not more ugly to the thing that helps it
> Than is my deed to my most painted word.
> O heavy burden!
>
> (Act 3, scene 1, 59 – 62)

The harlot can be seen as an allusion to Revelation 17:

Then one of the seven angels who were holding the seven bowls came to me and said: "Come, I will show you the judgment in store for the great harlot who sits by the waters of the deep."

(Rev 17, 1)

On her forehead was written a symbolic name, "Babylon the great, mother of harlots and all the world's abominations." I saw that the woman was drunk with the blood of God's holy ones and the blood of those martyred for their faith in in Jesus.

(Rev 17, 5-6)

Saint Patrick accuses Coroticus, a wolf on prowl, of leading the captive women away from God by selling them into slavery, in effect, consigning them to the brothel. Claudius compares himself to the harlot. He covers his blemishes, his evil deed; allegorically, he is Henry VIII, leading the English faithful away from God. Like the harlot of Babylon, the English Crown is drunk with the blood of the English martyrs.

Certain significant Biblical allusions appear in Hamlet's first soliloquy, in Act I, sc. 2:

> O, that this too, too sullied flesh would melt,
> Thaw, and resolve itself into a dew,
> Or that the Everlasting had not fixed
> His canon 'gainst (self-slaughter!) O God, God,
> How (weary,) stale, flat, and unprofitable
> Seem to me all the uses of this world!
> Fie on't, ah fie! 'Tis an unweeded garden

> That grows to seed. Things rank and gross in nature
> Possess it merely.

(Act 1, scene 2, 133 – 141)

The images in the first soliloquy, of dew and the unweeded garden, allude to Biblical passages, as does, later in the play, the Ghost's revelation of being poisoned as he slept in his orchard. In addition, the image of dew, as well as the garden imagery, relates profoundly to the allegorical meaning of the play.

The image of dew is associated with manna, the "bread which the Lord" gave to feed the Israelites for forty years in the desert.

> In the morning a dew lay all about the camp, and when the dew evaporated, there on the surface of the desert were fine flakes like hoarfrost on the ground. On seeing it, the Israelites asked one another, "What is this?" for they did not know what it was. But Moses told them, "This is the bread which the Lord has given you to eat."
>
> (Ex 16, 13 - 15)

The image of the "unweeded garden" echoes the Parable of the Weeds in Matthew 13:

> He proposed to them another parable: "The reign of God may be likened to a man who sowed good seed in his field. While every

one was asleep, his enemy came and sowed weeds through his
wheat, and then made off."

(Mt 13, 24 – 25)

Furthermore, the images of dew, of the unweeded garden,
and of the King sleeping in his garden, relate profoundly to a
command given by God to the Israelites:

> Moses said, "This is what the Lord has commanded. Keep an
> omerful of manna for your descendants, that they may see what
> food I gave you to eat in the desert when I brought you out of the
> land of Egypt." Moses then told Aaron, "Take an urn and put an
> omer of manna in it. Then place it before the Lord in safekeeping
> for your descendants." So Aaron placed it in front of the comand-
> ments for safekeeping, as the Lord had commanded Moses.

(Ex 16, 32 – 34)

The Lord commanded the Israelites to safeguard "the
bread which the Lord" gave. The manna from heaven prefig-
ures the Eucharist, which the Church in England, having broken with the Apostolic Authority of the Church and having
denounced the doctrine of Transubstantiation, had failed to
safeguard for its descendants, the English faithful.

King Hamlet, allegorically the Church's earthly head,
"slept" as his untended garden was invaded by those seeking
to sow the weeds of dissent. As in Matthew 13, while everyone
slept, the enemy came and sowed weeds through the wheat.

The enemy, the "serpent" who "stung" (1.5.43) the king in his garden, has poisoned the "bread which the Lord" gave. The "portion" was not safeguarded. In essence, the Church, having failed to reform, had slept as the Reformation took hold.

Moreover, Hamlet's hopelessness and despair, expressed in the metaphor of the unweeded garden, seem extreme, even considering his grief and disillusionment. Might Hamlet's reference to self-slaughter have some more metaphorical meaning, especially considering that resolving oneself into a "dew" seems an unlikely and odd description of suicide?

Is the playwright, through the persona of Hamlet, deploring his being in a state of spiritual death, in a world without grace? Is he accusing himself of committing spiritual suicide by not separating himself from the "rank" world of heresy? By remaining amongst the "weeds," has he thus failed to observe the canon of the Lord against self-slaughter?

The dew, the manna, the unweeded garden, might clearly be seen to direct us to the Gospel of John.

> "Let me firmly assure you,
> he who believes has eternal life.
> I am the bread of life.
> Your ancestors ate manna in the
>   desert, but they died.
> This is the bread that comes down
>   from heaven
> for a man to eat and never die.

I myself am the living bread
come down from heaven."

(John 6, 47 – 51)

"Let me solemnly assure you,
if you do not eat the flesh of the Son
      of Man
and drink his blood,
you have no life in you."

(John 6, 53)

As Hamlet, but perhaps the playwright, says at the end of the first soliloquy:

But break, my heart, for I must hold my tongue.

(Act 1, scene 2, 164)

Does the playwright, as yet not ready to speak, see himself and the English faithful, by their allowing themselves to be denied the "bread of life," as tacitly accepting the poison of heresy, as, therefore, being in compliance with heresy, and, as thus, committing spiritual "self-slaughter"?

A Biblical allusion in Hamlet's soliloquy in Act 2, scene 2, echoes the Lord's Servant in Isaiah 50. In his soliloquy, Hamlet accuses himself:

Am I a coward?

Who calls me "villain"? breaks my pate across?

Plucks off my beard and blows it in my face?

Tweaks me by the nose? gives me the lie i' th' throat …

(Act 2, scene 2, 598 - 601)

In Isaiah 50, the Lord's Servant speaks:

The Lord God has given me
a well-trained tongue,
That I might know how to speak to the
weary
a word that will rouse them.
Morning after morning
he opens my ear that I may hear;
And I have not rebelled,
have not turned back.
I gave my back to those who beat me,
my cheeks to those who plucked my
beard…

(Is 50, 4 – 6)

The Lord's Servant, knowing that God was his "help" and that he would not "be put to shame" (Is 50, 7), has stood firm, his face set "like flint," though others plucked his beard. Hamlet questions if he is a coward, who would allow another to insult him by such action as plucking his beard. In contrast to the Lord's Servant, who has not rebelled or turned back, who has used his well-trained tongue to rouse the weary, the speaker of the soliloquy, who has been commanded to set things right, accuses himself of saying nothing, of being "pigeon-livered" (2.2.604).

Is this voice, that of the speaker of the soliloquy, in fact the voice of the playwright, who knows that he has yet to speak, as a servant of the Lord, in defense of the Faith? The very evident Biblical allusion could make us think so.

Another passage that parallels certain Biblical texts, as well as *Confessio*, appears in Act 5, scene 2. Horatio, in effect, cautions Hamlet to obey his instincts if he is uncomfortable with the impending duel with Laertes. Hamlet responds:

> Not a whit. We defy augury. There is (a)
> special providence in the fall of a sparrow. If it be
> (now,) 'tis not to come; if it be not to come, it will be
> now; if it be not now, yet it (will) come. The
> readiness is all.

(Act 5, scene 2, 233 - 237)

The allusion to the sparrow is a reference to the Gospel of Matthew, Chapter 10:

> Are not
> two sparrows sold for next to nothing?
> Yet not a single sparrow falls to the
> ground without your Father's consent.
> As for you, every hair of your head

> has been counted; so do not be afraid
> of anything. You are worth more than
> an entire flock of sparrows.
>
> (Mt 10, 29 – 31)

In Matthew 10, Christ has given the Apostles the mission to go after "the lost sheep of the house of Israel" (Mt 10, 6). Christ says to them, "What I am doing is sending you out like sheep among wolves" (Mt 10, 16). He tells them to "give as a gift" (Mt 10, 8) the gift they have received.

The Apostles are instructed further:

> You yourselves will not be the speakers; the
> Spirit of your Father will be speaking in you.
>
> (Mt 10, 20)

As Sr. Declan points out (de Paor 106), Saint Patrick alludes to Matthew 10, 20 in the following passage in *Confessio;*

> *… and I believe that I was sustained by Christ my Lord,*
> *and that his Spirit was even then crying out on my behalf,*
> and I trust that will be so 'on the day of' my 'pressing need',
> as he affirms in the Gospel, '*On that day*',
> the Lord testifies: '*It is not you who speak*
> *but the SPIRIT of your Father is speaking in you.*'
>
> (C 20: 91- 96)

The Apostles trust in Christ as they carry out their mission to go after the lost sheep of Israel. Saint Patrick trusts that he is sustained by God: Father, Son, and Holy Spirit. Hamlet too trusts in the special providence of God who sees even the fall of a sparrow.

The mission of the Apostles and Saint Patrick is the same: to go after those who are lost to God. Is the playwright, speaking through Hamlet, also accepting a mission to go after those lost to the Faith in England?

Immediately after the reference to the fallen sparrow in Act 5, scene. 2, are lines that clearly echo lines in Habakkuk in the Old Testament. As already pointed out, Hamlet says to Horatio in Act 5, scene 2:

> If it be
>
> (now,) 'tis not to come; if it be not to come, it will be
> now; if it be not now, yet it (will) come. The
> readiness is all.
>
> (Act 5, scene 2, 234 - 237)

Habakkuk, Chapter 2:

> If it delays, wait for it,
> it will surely come, it will not be
> late.
>
> (Hb 2, 3)

The reason for the playwright's drawing attention to the Book of Habakkuk is evident when the quote is expanded:

I will stand at my guard post,
> and station myself upon the ram-
> > part,
And keep watch to see what he will
> > say to me,
and what answer he will give to my
> > complaint.
Then the Lord answered me and said:
> Write down the vision
Clearly upon the tablets,
> so that one can read it readily.
For the vision still has its time,
> > presses on to fulfillment, and will
> > > not disappoint;
If it delays, wait for it,
> > it will surely come, it will not be
> > > late.
The rash man has no integrity;
> > but the just man, because of his
> > > faith, shall live.

(Hb 2, 1-4)

Act 1 of the play echoes the prophet. The play opens with the guard at watch on the ramparts; the Ghost speaks, and Hamlet records his command in his memory, saying, "My tables – meet it is I set it down …" (1.5.114).

The play, in Act 5, scene 2, lines 234-237, quoted above, sounds distinctly, both in diction and rhythm, like Habakkuk 2, 3, also quoted above. It is more than evident that the play-wright has wanted to focus our attention on this particular text, first for the parallels between it and Act 1 of the play, but most especially, for an even more compelling reason.

Specifically, the line, "…but the just man, because of his faith, shall live," became a basis for Martin Luther's doctrine of justification by faith alone ("Great Texts of the Bible"). Luther asserted that man's salvation depended on his faith alone, not on both faith and good works. Luther's doctrine, thus at variance with Roman Catholicism and Eastern Christianity, became central to the Protestant Reformation.

In 1571, Church of England clerics, under the Ordination of Ministers Act 1571, were made to assent to the Thirty- Nine Articles of Religion. Article XI, Of the Justification of Man, states:

> We are accounted righteous before God, only for the merit of our
> Lord and Saviour Jesus Christ
> by Faith, and not for our own works or deservings….
>
> ("The 39 Articles of Religion")

The Council of Trent declared in 1547:

ON JUSTIFICATION

CANON IX. - If any one saith, that by faith alone the impious is justified; in such wise as to mean, that nothing else is required to co-operate in order to the obtaining the grace of Justification, and that it is not in any way necessary, that he be prepared and disposed by the movement of his own will; let him be anathema.

Session the Sixth

Celebrated on the thirteenth day of the month of January, 1547

("The Council of Trent")

The playwright has made a clearly deliberate effort to draw attention to this most crucial tenet of the Reformation. It is therefore imperative that we try to understand what he intends to communicate to us.

Critics would be free to assert that the playwright could be putting forth either the Catholic or the Protestant view, if it were not for the complex ties between Saint Patrick, the playwright, Matthew 10, and Habakkuk, all of which derive from one passage in the play. It is worth repeating the passage:

Not a whit. We defy augury. There is (a)
special providence in the fall of a sparrow. If it be
(now,) 'tis not to come; if it be not to come, it will be
now; if it be not now, yet it (will) come. The
readiness is all.

(Act 5, scene 2, 233 - 237)

The sparrow allusion in *Hamlet* leads us to both Matthew 10 and *Confessio*, with the reference to the Father speaking within both the Apostles and Saint Patrick. The remainder of the above quote then leads us directly to Habakkuk, where we encounter not only clear parallels to the play, but more significantly, where we confront the central doctrine of the Reformation.

Had the playwright not so purposefully in this quote led us to Saint Patrick before he directs us to Habakkuk, we might be free to allow some ambiguity about his intent. However, with that tie, in combination with all the other parallels between, and echoes of the writings of Saint Patrick, in *Hamlet*, we would be hard pressed not to see that the playwright intends to mean that he is in agreement with the Council of Trent.

PART TWO

THE PLAY AND
THE SOCIETY
OF JESUS

The allusions in *Hamlet* to the Jesuit Order, the parallels between the play and *The Spiritual Exercises of Saint Ignatius*, and the military references in the play clearly are intended to call to mind the Society of Jesus. The Jesuits played a significant role in the Counter-Reformation, and it is conceivable that the play, which so profoundly in its allegorical meaning defends the Faith, must also be recognized as making a major contribution to the mission of the Counter-Reformation. The playwright and the Jesuits were engaged in the same mission: defending the Faith and stopping the spread of heresy.

Saint Ignatius Loyola, who in his youth had been a soldier, founded the Society of Jesus in 1540. Members of the order were "expected to accept orders to go anywhere in the world," even to live in "extreme conditions" ("Society of Jesus"). The play opens with soldiers on watch, and closes with Fortinbras saying, "Go, bid the soldiers shoot." The Society of Jesus, whose members were "soldiers of God," strove "especially for the defence and propagation of the faith, and for the progress of souls in Christian life and doctrine" ("Society of Jesus").

The faculties of reason or intellect, conscience, and will are essential elements of both the play and *The Spiritual Exercises of Saint Ignatius*, which were developed by Ignatius to guide and instruct the person undertaking them in deepening his love of God, in serving God, and in gaining salvation. *The Exercises* guide the participant to think about, to contemplate, the life of Christ, to conduct a thorough examination of conscience, and to seek to discover God's will. Discernment of spirits, that is distinguishing which impulses to act are good and which are evil, is also a central element of *The Spiritual Exercises.*

The pattern of reason, conscience, will is equally evident in the play. It is made clear early in the play which characters have perception, reason, discernment. Hamlet is not only quick-witted, but also is highly perceptive. He has already discerned the true nature of Claudius before the action of the play begins. Ophelia perceives well the truth that Hamlet's vows are of heaven. However, her seemingly good intentions in obeying her father and avoiding Hamlet are not well-discerned, symbolically leading her away from that which is good. Gertrude, weak-willed and seduced by Claudius, does not see that he is but a "smiling, damned villain" (1.5.113) until Hamlet forces her to look upon him in contrast to the dead King. Claudius, the mighty opposite of Hamlet, equals him in perception, recognizing that Hamlet's brooding melancholy is "something in his soul" (3.1.178).

In the middle of the play, conscience and confession are central. The measure of each character's conscience is revealed. Hamlet's conscience is sterling, made clear by the number of sins of which he accuses himself in his encounter with Ophelia. Ophelia too has a strong conscience, evident when the Queen hopes that Ophelia's virtues will bring

Hamlet to his "wonted way again" (3.1.45). Polonius recognizes and admits his faulty judgment of Hamlet's intentions. Although Gertrude and Laertes, ruled by passion, persist too long in their belief in Claudius, both do repent, finally recognizing the falsehood of Claudius's "painted" words, too late, however, to save their lives. Only Claudius, burdened by his "rank" offense (3.3.40), exhibits self-knowledge and a conscience rivaling Hamlet's.

In addition to emphasizing reason and conscience, the play demonstrates the essentialness of will in distinguishing the characters. So much alike in both reason and conscience, Hamlet and Claudius are revealed to be truly opposite in respect to their will. Hamlet can turn his brains "[A]bout" (2.2.617), and, with the play within the play, recommit himself to the Ghost's command. Claudius, even on his knees, cannot give up the fruits of his crime, the crown and the Queen. Even more damning, when Gertrude has picked up the poisoned cup and Claudius still has time to prevent her drinking, he tells her only not to drink. Fully demonstrating the weakness of his will, he saves himself rather than Gertrude, by not revealing that the cup is poisoned.

Certain allusions (specifically the words "election" and "sealed") to the Jesuit Order and to the Pope, to whom Jesuits make a special vow of obedience, are evident in the exchange between Hamlet and Horatio just before the play within the play. A troupe of players has arrived at Elsinore. Hamlet has asked that they put on a play, "The Murder of Gonzago," and that a speech he will set down be inserted into the play.

Hamlet asks Horatio, to whom he has revealed the circumstances of his father's death, to observe the King to see if he shows signs of guilt when a scene resembling his father's murder is played. Hamlet says to Horatio, "Since my dear soul was mistress of her choice . . . her election / Hath sealed thee for herself" (3.2.68-69).

"Election" refers to *The Spiritual Exercises of Saint Ignatius*, to the Society of Jesus, and to the Pope; "sealed" can be seen as alluding to the Pope. *The Spiritual Exercises* guide one to control of passions, to clarity and detachment, in order to better discern and "elect" the paths that will lead one more fully to serve God. Echoing *The Exercises*, Hamlet has "elected" to trust Horatio because Horatio has control of his passions; in Horatio passion and reason are well-balanced, or, as Hamlet states, Horatio's "blood and judgment are so well / commedled . . ." (3.2.73-74). Furthermore, "election" alludes to the Pope, who is elected by the College of Cardinals, and to whom Jesuits make a special vow of obedience in their mission to save souls and spread the faith. Also, worn by the Pope is the Ring of the Fisherman, on which is the "Seal" of the Pope, the Pope's signet. As well, election alludes to the Superior General of the Jesuits who is elected by the General Congregation.

The two titles given to the play within the play are significant in calling our attention to the Jesuits, and to their role in the Counter-Reformation. The first of these titles, "The Murder of Gonzago," alludes both to the Jesuits, and to the House of Gonzaga, the ruling family of Mantua and other territory in Northern Italy. Of particular significance is one member of the family, Saint Aloysius Gonzaga, a young Jesuit who died of the plague in 1591, after helping to care for the sick in a hospital in Rome. He was beatified in 1605 by Pope Paul V, only fourteen years after his death. As will be discussed in Part Four, the playwright refers to the Gonzaga family in several other plays as well.

Hamlet calls the play within the play also by the title of "The Mousetrap." When he mistakenly kills Polonius, thinking it is Claudius, Hamlet refers to Claudius as a rat. The belief having been that rats spread the plague, calling Claudius a rat is the highest of insults. Moreover, the insult alluding to the plague could serve as further reference to Saint Aloysius Gonzaga, and thus to both the Jesuits and to the Gonzaga's.

Even more significant, however, is that the "mousetrap" is a metaphor used in a sermon by Saint Augustine of Hippo. The trap is the Cross; the bait is the death of Christ at which the Devil rejoices. However, Christ's Resurrection, the victory over death, defeats the Devil, who is thus ensnared by his own trap.

Claudius, too, is caught, ensnared in his guilt by "The Mousetrap," portraying before him his own crime. He is, furthermore, killed by the poison by which he had conspired to kill Hamlet, caught, like the Devil, in his own trap. Claudius is, as the Ghost has said, the serpent who wears his crown. Allegorically, Claudius, the "serpent", is Henry VIII who spread the poison of heresy.

The military references in the play bring to mind the Jesuits who, as soldiers of God, are defenders of the Faith. At the beginning of the play, soldiers are on watch on the ramparts. Bernardo comes at midnight to replace Francisco on the night watch. Bernardo asks, "Have you had quiet guard?" (1.1.10). Francisco replies, "Not a mouse stirring" (1.1.11). Only later in the play does it become apparent that the mouse is symbolically the Devil, and is allegorically Henry VIII. Allegorically, the soldiers on watch are, like the Jesuits, defending the Faith, and battling the spread of heresy.

The play, which has opened with soldiers on watch, closes with images of warfare and military ceremony.

Fortinbras commands:

> Let four captains
>
> Bear Hamlet like a soldier to the stage,
>
> For he was likely, had he been put on,
>
> To have proved most royal; and for his passage,
>
> The soldier's music and the rite of war. . .
>
> Speak loudly for him.
>
> Take up the bodies. Such a sight as this
>
> Becomes the field but here shows much amiss.
>
> Go, bid the soldiers shoot.
>
> (Act 5, scene 2, 441 - 449)

Hamlet is receiving full military honors. Allegorically, he has been engaged in spiritual warfare against heresy, in a battle for the souls of the English faithful. Hamlet's opponent, his mighty opposite, has been literally Claudius, but allegorically the Devil.

Likewise, the play portrays, allegorically, the playwright, the Jesuits, and the Church engaged in spiritual warfare, in a campaign, the Counter-Reformation, to reform, to defend the Faith, and to combat heresy.

PART THREE

PARALLELS: SAINT PATRICK AND THE PLAYWRIGHT

Saint Patrick relates certain aspects of himself in his works, several of which are paralleled in the characters of both Hamlet and Horatio in the play. The reader must wonder if these similar characteristics tell us something about the playwright himself.

I CONVERSION

As has been already discussed, both Saint Patrick and Horatio experience a conversion. Did the playwright as well?

II HESITATION

In *Confessio*, Saint Patrick tells of his hesitation in responding to the Spirit, in answering the call of God:

> *Whence moreover, I ought to give* unceasing *thanks to God,*
> Who has often pardoned *my lack of wisdom,*
> *and my negligence,*
> and who, on more than one occasion,
> refrained from growing vehemently angry with me,
> who had been chosen as his helper;
> and yet was slow to act in accordance with what I had
>   been shown,
> and as 'the Spirit was suggesting to me'...

(C 46: 125- 132)

He continues:

> . . .and I myself was slow to recognize *the grace* which was
>   then in me.
> Now I understand *what I ought* [*to have understood*] *earlier.*

> (C 46: 145–146)

Hamlet, as well, hesitates in his response to the Ghost's command. He berates himself, wondering if he is a coward (2.2.598).

In his soliloquy in Act 3, scene 1, Hamlet contemplates some evidently difficult decision:

> To be or not to be – that is the question:
> Whether 'tis nobler in the mind to suffer
> The slings and arrows of outrageous fortune,
> Or to take arms against a sea of troubles
> And, by opposing, end them. To die, to sleep –

> (Act 3, scene 1, 64–68)

Hamlet considers further:

>   To die, to sleep –
> To sleep, perchance to dream. Ay, there's the rub,
> For in that sleep of death what dreams may come,
> When we have shuffled off this mortal coil,
> Must give us pause.

> (Act 3, scene 1, 72–76)

Hamlet states that whether he should be, or not be, is the question. He questions whether it is more honorable to bear what fate brings, or more honorable to arm oneself against overwhelming troubles and thereby conquer them.

Hamlet repeats the line "To die, to sleep." The first "sleep" is perhaps avoidance of those troubles that fate may bring. Clearly the Church had slept, was not on watch, when the Reformation struck. The Church had avoided, had failed to reform, when it had erred. The Faith was not defended; the poison of heresy spread.

The second "sleep" is the sleep of death in which dreams may come. Might the second sleep, the sleep of death, be the afterlife? The second sleep, in death, may bring dreams good or bad, and thus must give us pause, must make us ponder, consider, judge, discern. Allegorically, in this sleep, the afterlife, might the good dreams be salvation, and the bad dreams be condemnation, spiritual death?

Hamlet continues:

> . . .The undiscovered country from whose bourn
> No traveler returns, puzzles the will
> And makes us rather bear those ills we have
> Than fly to others that we know not of?
> Thus conscience does make cowards (of us all,) ...
>
> (Act 3, scene 1, 87 – 91)

The undiscovered country to which one might go to escape the ills that fortune brings is unknown, no traveler there having returned. Therefore, one loses the will to go there, in other words, chooses to accept what fate brings rather than face the unknown future to rid oneself of those ills.

Hamlet says of thinking too much:

> ...And thus the native hue of resolution
> Is (sicklied) o'er with the pale cast of thought,
> And enterprises of great pitch and moment
> With this regard their currents turn awry
> And lose the name of action.
>
> (Act 3, scene 1, 92 – 96)

Might Hamlet, but actually the playwright, be questioning if he sleeps, if he does not, symbolically, take up arms against the Reformation, will his sleep in death bring bad dreams, in other words, bring condemnation?

Has the playwright, like Saint Patrick, hesitated in responding to the Spirit? Does he berate himself, call himself a coward, delay in answering the call to action, the call to vindicate, to write in defense of the Faith? Has he lost his will to act as a result of thinking too much about this decision of whether to be, or not to be?

Saint Patrick explains that he had long thought about writing *Confessio,* but had hesitated:

> On which account *I have* long since *thought* about writing,
> but 'until now' I hesitated;
> for I feared lest '*I should fall under the censure of the tongue*'
>   *of people,*
> because *I have not learned* 'just as others'…

(C 9: 1- 4)

Saint Patrick has described in his writing his hesitation in answering God's call, and his thinking too much about, and therefore his hesitation in, writing *Confessio*. Is it perhaps likely that the playwright describes in *Hamlet* the same hesitation and the same thinking too much about the taking of similar action? Saint Patrick attributes his hesitancy to write to his being unschooled, unlearned. The playwright expresses in Hamlet's soliloquy that too much thinking about, too much awareness of what may come prevents action, makes cowards of us. Is the enterprise of "great pitch and moment" the writing of the plays, an action that could bring retribution, accusation of treason, even death, if the Crown saw itself attacked?

III   CANNOT REMAIN SILENT

n *Confessio*, Saint Patrick states:

> Whence moreover I cannot remain silent,
> 'nor indeed is it expedient' [that I should],
> concerning such great benefits
> and the great grace
> which the Lord has been pleased to bestow on me
> 'IN THE LAND OF MY CAPTIVITY',
> because this is what we can give in return
> after God corrects us and brings us to know him:
> 'TO EXALT AND CONFESS HIS WONDROUS DEEDS
> before every nation
> which is under every heaven.'
>
> (C 3: 1- 11)

In his first soliloquy, in Act 1, scene 2, having compared the world to an "unweeded garden," and having expressed his condemnation of his mother's marriage to Claudius, Hamlet concludes by stating:

But break, my heart, for I must hold my tongue.

(Act 1, scene 2, 164)

Only through the play within the play will Hamlet later be able to give voice to the heinousness of the offense. Only through the play itself will the playwright be able to vindicate, to defend against heresy, to remind the English faithful of spiritual truth that was tainted by the Reformation.

IV LEGACY

Saint Patrick, inspired by God to serve the pagan people in Ireland, and granted the flock of faithful con-
verts, intends that *Confessio* be his legacy to them. He states:

> ... that at last WITH HUMILITY and in truth *I might serve them.*
> And so, 'according to the measure of the faith' of the
>> Trinity it is my duty,
> *without fear of the censure* [*I may incur*],
> *to make known 'THE GIFT OF GOD'*
> and [his] 'eternal consolation';
> *without fear*
> faithfully *to expound everywhere the name of God,*
> *so that* even 'after my death' *I may leave behind a legacy to my*
>> *brethren and children,*
> whom I have baptized in the Lord ...

> (C 13-14: 70- 78)

At the end of the play, Hamlet, dying, charges Horatio to vindicate him, to make the truth known:

> Horatio, I am dead.
> Thou livest; report me and my cause aright
> To the unsatisfied.

> (Act 5, scene 2, 370 - 372)

Horatio, calling himself more an "antique Roman" than a Dane picks up the poisoned cup. Hamlet, demanding that Horatio give him the cup, continues:

> O God, Horatio, what a wounded name,
> Things standing thus unknown, shall I leave behind
>   me!
> If thou didst ever hold me in thy heart,
> Absent thee from felicity awhile
> And in this harsh world draw thy breath in pain
> To tell my story.

> (Act 5, scene 2, 378 – 384)

Horatio, the poisoned cup taken from him, will assume, even under painful conditions, the role of fulfilling the Ghost's command. Horatio, but, in reality, the playwright, will tell the story that sets things right, that vindicates, that makes things whole. Like Saint Patrick, the playwright will leave a legacy, will serve the faithful by conveying truth.

V HAMLET, HORATIO, FORTINBRAS: ONE MISSION

In *Confessio*, Saint Patrick, who has spread Christianity in Ireland, states his desire to "strengthen and confirm" the faith of his brethren (C 47: 149). The playwright's mission is essentially the same: to reaffirm traditional Christian belief, and to strengthen the faith of believers.

By the end of the play, Hamlet, Horatio, and Fortinbras have all committed to carrying out the Ghost's command. Allegorically, the command is to vindicate, to set things right. The command has called the three characters to the one mission, allegorically, the mission of the Counter-Reformation: to reform the Church, to defend the Faith, and to stop the spread of heresy.

Hamlet enlists Horatio to report the cause "aright." Horatio will tell the story. Fortinbras, back from a successful military campaign, will take command. At the end, Horatio and Fortinbras join forces to place the bodies high on a stage to convey to the "yet unknowing world" (5.2.421) the story of how such carnage has come about, so that further "plots and errors" (5.2.440) might not happen. Allegorically, is the story that of the Reformation? Is the carnage the effect of the Reformation on the Church and the faithful? Is Horatio, at the end, the playwright who will "tell the story," and is Fortinbras, in a position of command, the head of the Church, the Pope, or the head of the Jesuit Order, its Superior General? Has the play portrayed the poet, the Jesuits, and the Church joined together in the mission to set right the time that is "out of joint?"

Early in the play, Hamlet can be seen as prophetic. Not yet having heard the Ghost's revelations, he suspects Claudius of foul play.

Is Horatio's name an allusion to the Roman poet Horace, the leading lyric poet in the reign of Emperor Augustus, during whose reign Christ was born? Do we hear through the voices of Hamlet and Horatio the voice of the playwright, poet and prophet, as he evolves from skepticism to belief, from suspicion to awareness, from hesitation to action, from doubt to trust, and finally from avoidance to acceptance of his mission?

When Hamlet asks Horatio, whom he trusts and whom he has brought fully into his confidence, to observe Claudius for signs of guilt during the play within the play, he, in effect, commissions Horatio to aid in the mission of obeying the Ghost's command. After Hamlet's death,

Horatio will continue the mission; he will be the voice of both poet and prophet. The two characters have merged accordingly into one voice: that of the playwright.

At the end of the play, Horatio is fully committed to the mission. He states to Fortinbras and to the Ambassadors from England, newly arrived at the castle:

> You from the Polack wars, and you from England,
> Are here arrived, give order that these bodies
> High on a stage be placed to the view
> And let me speak to (th') yet unknowing world
> How these things came about. So shall you hear
> Of carnal, bloody, and unnatural acts,
> Of accidental judgments, casual slaughters,
> Of deaths put on by cunning and (forced) cause,
> And, in this upshot, purposes mistook
> Fall'n on th' inventors' heads. All this can I
> Truly deliver
>
> (Act 5, scene 2, 418 – 428)

Hamlet dies, prophesying that Fortinbras will assume command:

> O, I die, Horatio,
> The potent poison quite o'ercrows my spirit.
> I cannot live to hear the news from England.
> But I do prophesy th' election lights
> On Fortinbras; he has my dying voice.

So tell him, with th' occurrents, more and less,

Which have solicited – the rest is silence.

(Act 5, scene 2, 389 – 395)

Fortinbras, whose name means strong arm, a combination of the French word for "strong" (forte) and of the French word for "arm" (le bras), accepts his position:

For me, with sorrow I embrace my fortune.

I have some rights of memory in this kingdom,

Which now to claim my vantage doth invite me.

(Act 5, scene 2, 431 – 433)

On the literal level, it is assumed that Fortinbras will take up the crown of Denmark. The unexpected use of the word "election" in this context should imply to us that something more significant is intended, on the allegorical level. Might Fortinbras represent the Pope, the next successor to Peter, to be elected by the College of Cardinals? Or, might the playwright be telling us that, allegorically, Hamlet is prophesying that Fortinbras will be the next Superior General of the Society of Jesus? Election by the General Congregation was the method instituted by Ignatius for selecting the head of the Jesuit Order.

Fortinbras has just returned from a successful "military" campaign in Poland. The role of the Jesuits in helping to control the spread of Protestantism in the Polish-Lithuanian Commonwealth and in southern Germany during the Counter-Reformation was significant ("Society of Jesus").

As well, Fortinbras, he of strong arm, represents what Christianity traditionally referred to as the Church militant (Ecclesia militans), all the faithful on earth, in contrast to the Church triumphant, those in heaven. As a result of their waging war against sin, evil, and the powers of darkness, the faithful on earth were called militant, soldiers of Christ.

Fortinbras's speech at the very end of the play echoes both military ceremony and a military campaign. Fortinbras accords military honor to Hamlet.

> Let four captains
> Bear Hamlet like a soldier to the stage,
> For he was likely, had he been put on,
> To have proved most royal; and for his passage,
> The soldier's music and the rite of war
> Speak loudly for him.
> Take up the bodies. Such a sight as this
> Becomes the field but here shows much amiss.
> Go, bid the soldiers shoot.

(Act 5, scene 2, 441 - 449)

The military references allude to the Society of Jesus, instrumental in the Church's effort to defend the Faith and to counter heresy during the Counter-Reformation. They allude as well to the Church militant.

The play ends with Hamlet, Horatio, and Fortinbras having united in spiritual warfare, in the mission to carry out the Ghost's command. Fortinbras, defender of the Faith, gives command in the last line of the play to engage in battle. Speaking through Hamlet and Horatio is the voice of the playwright, poet and prophet, who will, like the Servant of the Lord in Isaiah, speak with a well-trained tongue to rouse the faithful.

The playwright has committed to the mission. He has taken up "arms," joined forces with the Jesuit Order and the Church, and with his pen will recruit the faithful to engage in the campaign against heresy.

Moreover, the playwright has defined the mission. The Ghost's command to vindicate is the mission of the Counter-Reformation. The playwright has spoken well: the play has indeed set things right; it has shown what is true; it has defended the Faith; it has vindicated.

The play is truly for all ages and all time, its message as needed today as it was in past centuries. The play portrays the human flaws, the Church that had erred and those in protest who had usurped, that led to the "heinous" offenses. As did Saint Patrick in his letter to Coroticus, the playwright expresses hope that those who offended, (those who had erred and those who had usurped), would return to their senses and be made whole.

PART FOUR

THE QUESTION
OF AUTHORSHIP

The very evident links between the ancient writings of Saint Patrick and *Hamlet* can perhaps give us some insights into the authorship of the play.

Horatio, poet, will tell the story. The playwright does tell the story, his legacy to the faithful, to defend, to justify the "wounded name" of the Faith.

Like Saint Patrick, the playwright has a mission. Like Saint Patrick, the playwright, if indeed represented by the merging of the voices of Hamlet and Horatio, undergoes conversion, hesitates, ultimately cannot remain silent, and finally, leaves, for the ages, a legacy, a confession of what he holds to be spiritual truth.

Given the evidence, we can presume that the playwright had familiarity with the ancient writings of Saint Patrick. We also can presume, given the parallels and allusions to the Society of Jesus, that the playwright had knowledge of, if not connection to, the Jesuit Order and its precepts, and that he was familiar with *The Spiritual Exercises of Saint Ignatius*.

Richard Paul Roe, in his work, *The Shakespeare Guide to Italy*, maintains that whoever wrote the plays had significant first-hand knowledge of Italy. A lawyer, Roe traveled extensively in Italy, following the clues of textual evidence in the plays. He states in the preface to his work:

> In truth, as will be demonstrated, the precise and abundant
> allsions in those plays to places and things the length of that
> country are so unique to it that they attest to the playwright's per
> sonal travels there. By journeying in Italy today, with the Italian
> plays in hand, reading them as though they were books of instruc
> tion, the playwright's vast erudition about that exciting country
> and its civilization is revealed.
>
> (Roe 1)

With the abundant evidence that Roe presents for ten of the thirteen plays set in Italy, we would be hard-pressed not to agree with his conclusions.

In addition to the other attributes of Saint Patrick already discussed, Patrick reveals in *Confessio* still more about himself. In Part I, he refers to himself being "among an alien people." In Part III, he terms Ireland, where he has proclaimed the Gospel, the "limit beyond which nobody dwells." He refers also to his loss of "country and kindred," and his having surrendered his "freeborn status for the benefit of others." In Part IV, he declares that he has chosen to remain in Ireland "until I die."

It is interesting to consider that if the playwright seems clearly to identify with Saint Patrick's conversion, his hesitation, his not being able to remain silent, and his leaving a legacy of words, might the playwright also identify with Patrick being an alien, with his being in a remote country, with his loss of country and family, and with his giving up of status?

It is interesting, as well, to speculate who the playwright might be, if not the Bard of Stratford. Although there is speculation that Shakespeare may have been a recusant Catholic, he is believed not to have traveled abroad. Edward de Vere, 17th Earl of Oxford, is believed, at a point in his life, to have had Catholic leanings, and did spend extended time in Italy. However, he returned to England, and gave up neither country nor title.

Christopher Marlowe, on the other hand, would perfectly parallel Saint Patrick, if, as the Marlovians contend, he faked his death in Deptford in order to escape the Privy Council, if he was a double agent, converted to the Catholic cause, if he lived a life of exile in an alien country, perhaps Italy. He would have given up his status as an acclaimed London playwright, and would have dispatched his plays back to England, just as Saint Patrick dispatched to England his *Epistola,* to be read before Coroticus. His legacy would have been, not his fame, but like Saint Patrick's, a testament to faith.

Might he even have identified with Saint Patrick's closing words in *Confessio*?

> But I beseech those who believe in
> and fear God,
> whoever is pleased to look at
> or receive this writing….

(C 62: 1 – 4)

> ... if I have accomplished or demonstrated any small thing
> according to God's good pleasure;
> but let this be your conclusion and it must be most truly
>> believed
> that it was 'THE GIFT OF GOD'.
> And this is my Confession
> before I die.

(C 62: 7-12)

In *The Shakespeare Guide to Italy*, Richard Paul Roe offers several details of particular interest in relation to both the meaning and the authorship of the plays. Of the thirteen plays set in Italy, he discusses ten in which the action takes place in the Middle Ages or the Renaissance.

In Chapter 3, Roe notes a reference to a Friar Patrick in *The Two Gentlemen of Verona*. The friar, who does not actually appear as a character in the play, is merely mentioned in the context of a character, Sylvia, going to his cell for "holy confession" (Roe 80).

As the play is set in Italy, the name Patrick seems oddly out of place. For a second time in one of his plays, the playwright has drawn our attention to the name Patrick, and thus conceivably to the writings of Saint Patrick, and, as well, to the allegorical meaning of the play.

Roe suggests that the playwright was alluding to an Irish Franciscan friar named Patrick O'Hely (Roe 80). In 1576, O'Hely was named Bishop of Mayo by Pope Gregory XIII, and in 1579 was hanged for his supposed role in a plot against English control in Ireland, in defense of the Faith. In 1992, Patrick O'Hely was beatified by Pope John Paul II, and is considered one of a group of Irish Martyrs.

In Chapter 8, Roe contends that the setting for *A Midsummer Night's Dream* is a town called Sabbioneta, twenty-five miles southwest of Mantua (Roe 186). The founder of this town, Vespasiano Gonzaga, had been educated at the Royal Court of Spain, had served Philip II of Spain as a general, and was a member of a branch of the House of Gonzaga that ruled the Duchy of Mantua. Moreover, Vespasiano was a patron of the arts, who collected art and sculpture, and who created in his model town, a gathering place for scholars and cultivated guests. As Roe points out, the town thus earned the nickname *La Piccola Atena*, or "Little Athens." He provides evidence to support his argument that it is this Athens, and not Athens in Greece, that is the setting for *A Midsummer Night's Dream*, and conjectures that the playwright "may well have been invited" there (Roe 186).

It is interesting to note that the House of Gonzaga is alluded to not only in *Hamlet* and *A Midsummer Night's Dream*, but also in *The Taming of the Shrew*. As Roe states in Chapter 4 of *The Shakespeare Guide to Italy*, in a conversation between Tranio and the Mercantant in *The Taming of the Shrew*, Mantua is mentioned three times. The Duke of Mantua, a member of the Gonzaga family that had ruled Mantua since 1328, is referred to as well. Roe notes also that the playwright has alluded to Mantua having a fleet of ships.

As Roe points out, it was a "substantial fleet of both merchant ships, and ships of war, fully capable of plying the Po, the Adige, the Adriatic, and far beyond" (Roe 110).

Not only did the Gonzaga family produce Saint Aloysius Gonzaga, a Jesuit priest, but also twelve cardinals and fourteen bishops. The very significant and very pointed allusions by the playwright to this family, and its ships, should make us question what the Gonzaga's relationship to the playwright might have been, and what role, if any, they might have played in getting the plays to the English stage.

It is interesting to speculate. If the playwright was Edward de Vere, might he have had contact with the Gonzaga's during his travels in Italy? Or, if Marlowe was the playwright, might he have been spirited out of England aboard a Gonzaga ship? Might Marlowe, on Gonzaga ships, have dispatched plays from Italy back to England?

If indeed Shakespeare was not the author of the plays, but did introduce them to the English stage, he would have been a most significant player in a highly dangerous plot. His role in the mission to defend the Faith would have placed him in a most crucial and most perilous position. If the plays had been deemed treasonous, it is Shakespeare who would have been martyred.

In the final analysis, what we know with certainty is that there are very clear and distinct parallels between *Hamlet* and Saint Patrick's ancient texts. We know also that there are significant parallels to *The Spiritual Exercises of Saint*

Ignatius. We know that whoever wrote the plays had considerable knowledge of Italy, and that he very purposefully draws our attention, for some reason, to the Gonzaga family. The playwright has thus given us well-chosen and very deliberate clues to unlock both his meaning and perhaps his identity as well.

BIBLIOGRAPHY

Cahill, Thomas. *How the Irish Saved Civilization*. New York: Doubleday, 1995.

De Paor, Marie B. *PATRICK The Pilgrim Apostle of Ireland*. New York: Harper Collins Publishing, 1998.

"Great Texts of the Bible." Bible Hub, 2004-2021, https://www.biblehub.com/commentaries/hastings/Habakkuk/2 -4htm.

Greenblatt, Stephen. *Hamlet in Purgatory*. Princeton, New Jersey: Princeton University Press, 2001.

Knight, Wilson. *The Wheel of Fire*. 1930. London: Routledge, 1989.

Loyola, Ignatius. *The Spiritual Exercises of Saint Ignatius*, translated by Anthony Mottola. New York: Doubleday, 1964.

New American Bible. New York: Catholic Book Publishing Co., 1970.

Roe, Richard Paul. *The Shakespeare Guide to Italy*. New York: Harper Collins Publishing, 2011.

Shakespeare, William. *SHAKESPEARE Twenty-three Plays and the Sonnets*, edited by Thomas Marc Parrot. New York: Charles Scribner's Sons, 1953.

Shakespeare, William. *The Tragedy of HAMLET, Prince of Denmark*, edited by Barbara A. Mowat, and Paul Werstine. New York: Washington Square Press, 1992.

Shapiro, James. *CONTESTED WILL Who Wrote Shakespeare?*. New York: Simon & Schuster, Inc, 2010.

"Society of Jesus." Wikipedia, Wikimedia Foundation, 29 June 2021, https://en.wikipedia.org/Wiki/Society _ of _ Jesus.

"The Council of Trent." Hanover Historical Texts Project, 1995, https://history. hanover.edu/texts/trentall.html.

"The 39 Articles of Religion." Victorian Web, 19 June 2018, www.victorianweb.org/religion/39articles.html.

"Thirty-nine Articles." Wikipedia, Wikimedia Foundation, 6 July 2021, https://en.wikipedia.org/wiki/Thirty-nine _ Articles.

"Wives of Henry VIII." Wikipedia, Wikimedia Foundation, 17 June 2021, https://en.wikipedia.org/Wiki/Wives _ of _ Henry _ VIII.

ABOUT THE AUTHOR

Returning to the classroom after raising a family, Patricia Geaney Kerrigan was fortunate to teach twelfth graders, whose curriculum included *Hamlet*. Her passion for the play and her conviction of its allegorical meaning grew each year. In retirement, her continued interest in the play has resulted in *HAMLET In Defense of the Faith*, in which she explores the connection between the play and two ancient texts. Patricia and her husband live in Massachusetts. She enjoys spending time with her grandchildren, reading, gardening, and traveling. Having grown up an Army Brat, she considers many places to be home.

Made in United States
North Haven, CT
01 June 2024

53187561R00082